To:

From:

Date:

3-MINUTE DEVOTIONS
for a
Heart-Shaped Life

KAREN MOORE

BARBOUR BOOKS
An Imprint of Barbour Publishing, Inc.

Published by Barbour Books, an imprint of Barbour Publishing, Inc., 1810 Barbour Drive, Uhrichsville, Ohio 44683, www.barbourbooks.com

Our mission is to inspire the world with the life-changing message of the Bible.

Member of the
Evangelical Christian
Publishers Association

Printed in the United States of America.

A Heart-Shaped Life!

These devotions were written especially for those moments when you need a little reminder that you are a recipient of the fullness of God's goodness and love. A little inspiration each day helps to change your perspective and lighten your heart to make life's journey easier. As it says in Proverbs 4:23 (MSG), "Keep vigilant watch over your heart; *that's* where life starts."

Just three tiny minutes is all you'll need to be well on your way to a heart-shaped life.

- ♥ Minute 1: Read the day's Bible verse and reflect on its meaning.
- ♥ Minute 2: Read the devotion and think about its application for your life.
- ♥ Minute 3: Pray.

Although these devotions aren't meant as a tool for deep Bible study, they can be a touch point to keep you grounded and focused on God, who is Love Himself. May every moment you spend with this book be a blessing!

Dear children, let us not love with words or speech but with actions and in truth.
1 JOHN 3:18 NIV

Dedication

*For every reader who knows that nothing is more
important than precious moments spent with God.
May you be blessed beyond measure.*
–Karen Moore

In the Spirit of Love

*Follow God's example, therefore, as dearly loved
children and walk in the way of love, just as
Christ loved us and gave himself up for us as
a fragrant offering and sacrifice to God.*
EPHESIANS 5:1–2 NIV

As we develop a spirit of love and grow more confident in our walk with the Lord, this passage from Ephesians invites us to imitate Jesus. He is someone we want to be close to and someone we love. We want to please Him in every possible way, and we want to have Him see that we are "growing up" in faith.

As you put on a spirit of love today, see if you can imitate Jesus, be like Him in some special way, or be more like Him in a way that hasn't been easy for you in the past. . .more giving, more compassionate, or more patient. Follow Him wherever you go today!

*Lord, help me to put on childlike faith in You
today, imitating Your love for others and
creating a spirit of peace within my
soul. Bless all I do this day. Amen.*

The Apple of His Eye

For the LORD's portion is his people, Jacob his allotted
inheritance. . . . He shielded him and cared for him;
he guarded him as the apple of his eye.

DEUTERONOMY 32:9–10 NIV

You might remember that Jacob was shielded and cared for by God's grace. He was guarded and protected. What joy it is to remember that we are cared for in the same way! We are shielded from things we don't even know He protected us from. We are cared for by angels with tender mercy wherever we happen to be. Why? Because we're loved so much!

When you feel good about yourself, you extend more mercy and love to others. If the Lord's portion is His people, then you are the reason He has joy, for you are one of His beloved. See each person you meet today as the "apple of God's eye"! When you do, you'll see more clearly that each one is worthy of great love.

Lord, let me act today as though I understand
what it truly means to be the "apple" of Your
eye. Let me know Your protection, mercy,
and love in all that comes my way. Amen.

Loving the Unlovable

"To you who are ready for the truth, I say this: Love your enemies. . . . No more tit-for-tat stuff. Live generously."

LUKE 6:27, 30 MSG

Sometimes you treat others with kindness and they still throw you under the bus or tell lies about you. It's possible that even your friends will betray you. When those things happen and your heart is broken, it's not easy to do it God's way. However, the scripture answer is pretty clear, "Love, do good, bless, and pray."

Abusive actions of others give us no excuse to be abusive in return. Instead, we are given opportunities in difficult moments to put Jesus into action, to show God's love, even if we can't quite show our own. May you find that your heart is so shaped by God's love that you can even embrace those who appear to be unlovable.

*Lord, let me out-love all those around me today.
Let me be an example of Your care, Your gifts,
and Your presence wherever I am. Amen.*

Joyful, Patient, Faithful. . .Me?

Be joyful because you have hope. Be patient
when trouble comes, and pray at all times.
Share with God's people who need help.
ROMANS 12:12-13 NCV

When affliction comes, sometimes we lose our ability or our desire to pray. We wonder if God is still near. What do we do then?

The writer of Romans gives us a suggestion. When our hope is down, we can turn our attention to others. We can share with God's people in need and practice hospitality. We can take the opportunity to volunteer our services and our talents and take our minds away from our lagging spirits. In so doing, we may discover that hope returns. Giving from the heart produces wings of hope. Giving of ourselves brings patience and peace.

Remember that you are an ambassador of hope because you have the love of Jesus tucked inside your soul. Let your heart return to that hope today.

Lord, renew my hope today. Let my spirits rise
as I work, live, and serve others in Your name.
Let my heart find hope in You again. Amen.

Please Pass the Salt

"Salt is good for seasoning. But if it loses its flavor, how do you make it salty again? You must have the qualities of salt among yourselves and live in peace with each other."

MARK 9:50 NLT

What would happen if you added salt to your favorite dish, but it remained bland? What if it had no taste at all?

This passage from Mark reminds us that we as Christians are the "salt." We're the salty spice, the ones who enhance life and flavor it with joy. It's the salt of God's love and of the Holy Spirit that helps flavor our lives and those of others as well. The right amount of salt, the kind you carry in your heart and your spirit, helps you bring the best out of each person you meet.

The best way for others to see how desirable your faith is, is if you're willing to share. Come on, don't be bland—spice things up and pass the salt!

Lord, let me show Your Spirit in ways that flavor the lives of those around me. Help me truly be the "salt" that adds to the goodness of life. Amen.

Do You Really Know What Time It Is?

Do not forget this one thing, dear friends: With the Lord a day is like a thousand years, and a thousand years are like a day. The Lord is not slow in keeping his promise, as some understand slowness. Instead he is patient with you.

2 PETER 3:8–9 NIV

We're all driven by the clock. We're in a hurry to get up, get to work, get the job done, get home, feed the kids, get to the store, get to Bible study, or watch our favorite TV show and then get to bed and start all over again. Whatever it is that we have to do or wherever it is we have to be, we're in a hurry to get there.

Today, God seems to be saying, "Don't worry and don't hurry." If we believe that God is in the details of our lives, then we can afford to be a little more patient with others and with ourselves. As you stand in the endless lines of life, allow for His perfect timing, pray for inner peace, and be gracious. It will do your heart good.

Lord, remind me that my time is always Yours. Let me move in the rhythm of Your divine timing for all that You would have me accomplish today. Amen.

Matters of the Heart

And be kind to one another, tenderhearted,
forgiving one another, even as God
in Christ forgave you.
EPHESIANS 4:32 NKJV

Compassion is one of those words that gets to the heart of the matter quickly. It is only needed when a situation is out of control. . .too much sorrow, too little money, too much need. . .it goes on and on. We prefer to share our compassionate hearts more than we want to be the recipients of other people's compassion. Yet life happens to us all and, at one time or another, we each need the kindness, compassion, and forgiveness of someone else.

Today, make it your primary goal to have a soft heart, one that is kinder and more compassionate to everyone you meet. God is working with each of us, to give us more tender hearts.

Lord, let me give from a heart of compassion, act with
a desire toward kindness, and extend the hand
of forgiveness to those I meet today. Amen.

Who's My Neighbor?

*"Then the King will say to those on his right, 'Enter, you
who are blessed by my Father! Take what's coming to you
in this kingdom. It's been ready for you since the world's
foundation. And here's why: I was hungry and you fed me,
I was thirsty and you gave me a drink, I was homeless
and you gave me a room, I was shivering and you
gave me clothes, I was sick and you stopped to
visit, I was in prison and you came to me.' "*

MATTHEW 25:35–36 MSG

God is pleased when you help in whatever ways you can
to care for your community and your family. He asks you
to care for others in the same way Jesus cares about you.

The world is shrinking. Your neighbors are no longer simply living on your same street or your same town.
They live across the country, across the continent, and
around the world. You have endless opportunities to
show kindness and to give encouragement and love. God
blesses those acts—the big ones and the small ones—and
fills your heart with joy in the things you do to share His
love with others.

Today, may you realize that every act of kindness,
every word of encouragement, and every good deed you
do makes the heart of your Father burst with joy.

*Lord, let me offer a kind heart and a compassionate
word to any who might need me to strengthen
and nourish their souls today. Amen.*

A Heart for Sharing

Make sure you don't take things for granted and go slack
in working for the common good; share what you have with
others. God takes particular pleasure in acts of worship—
a different kind of "sacrifice"—that take place in
kitchen and workplace and on the streets.
HEBREWS 13:16 MSG

In the race between good and evil, most people have the intention of being good and of being generous to others. If we open our hearts to that notion, God will continue to instruct us and give us guidance about how we can do good deeds in a variety of ways. He will lighten our hearts and give us joy. He will bless our efforts and make us glad.

May God help you have a heart for others in some very new ways today. Whether you bake brownies for the new neighbors, encourage a coworker, or give a generous tip to the waiter at lunch, God will see your work . . .and your heart!

Lord, help me to recognize those who need
me in some special way today. Amen.

You Are So Kind!

Love suffers long and is kind; love does not envy; love does
not parade itself, is not puffed up; does not behave rudely,
does not seek its own, is not provoked, thinks no evil;
does not rejoice in iniquity, but rejoices in the
truth; bears all things, believes all things,
hopes all things, endures all things.
1 CORINTHIANS 13:4–7 NKJV

Doing kind things gives you a glimpse of the way your heart is shaped by God. You can see how He causes you to think about others first and imagine what He is trying to accomplish in their lives. You see His light glow as a little ember in each person you encounter.

You know the kindness God holds toward you and all of His creation. Breathe it in. Share it. Be kind and shine the light of God's love on those in need. You'll find them waiting for you every place you go. You'll find that you have more spring in your step and a song in your heart when you let kindness lead the way.

Lord, when I forget to reach out, when I am too busy to
lend a hand, or when I no longer have a moment to
shine Your light, then be patient with me. Amen.

It's Time to Party

*For seven days celebrate the festival to the LORD your God
at the place the LORD will choose. For the LORD your God
will bless you in all your harvest and in all the work
of your hands, and your joy will be complete.*
DEUTERONOMY 16:15 NIV

God is the Creator of just plain fun, just as much as He is
the Creator of all the other aspects of our humanity. Our
days are quickly passing. We're moving at an incredible
pace, doing, doing, and still doing!

Listen for God's voice today and see if He isn't nudg-
ing you, in fact, urging you to stop and take some time
apart and discover the joy in your good work. See if He
doesn't want you to simply celebrate all the good things
He's already brought into your life. Maybe today is the
day you pop into the local bakery, grab a sweet delight,
and invite God to share it with you.

Are you listening? Are you having fun yet?

*Lord, help me to listen for the right moments to just
live it up. . .that is, live in an upbeat, joyful way
for all that You've done for me. Amen.*

Just as You Believe

Then Jesus said to the Roman officer,
"Go on home. What you have believed has happened!"
And the boy was healed that same hour!
MATTHEW 8:13 TLB

When trials come or the limits of our faith are tested, our strength wavers. We question whether God is listening or even what it means to be faithful. Our hearts need more encouragement. Our minds need comfort and more instruction.

According to the Bible story, the centurion reached Jesus after offering his own prayers and making an effort on behalf of his servant. When his own efforts failed, he went straight to the Source. He didn't give room for the idea that Jesus might not be able to help. He just believed that Jesus could save his servant. *He just believed it!*

Believe it! Your life can change too. . .with God's help. You do not have to rely on your own strength. Put all you are and all you want to be in God's hand today.

Lord, please help me to keep believing and to
be trusting. Help me to be faithful today. Amen.

Child of God

*And the Spirit himself joins with our spirits
to say we are God's children.*
ROMANS 8:16 NCV

When you were born into God's family, you started taking on a resemblance to your spiritual family. Perhaps angels said, "She has her Father's eyes, her Creator's gift for joy, or her Savior's gift of grace. She has a heart for God." It was another scene where love was happening at first sight.

God never makes you wonder who your Father is, for He testifies within you, establishing Himself in your spirit, to let you know that you are His. He wants very much for you to have your Father's heart and your Father's love. He wants you to be a spitting image of Him.

May your Father's heart guide you in all you do today so that others may see Him reflected in your face.

Lord, thanks for reminding me that I am Your child and that You have already claimed me in Your love. Amen.

Divine Discipline

*No discipline seems pleasant at the time, but painful.
Later on, however, it produces a harvest of righteousness
and peace for those who have been trained by it.*
HEBREWS 12:11 NIV

Discipline of any sort is not easy. During Lent, you may try not to eat chocolate, or at the New Year you may make a commitment to exercise or to be more consistent about your prayer life. As children of God, we sometimes need reminders of His hopes and expectations for us. Those reminders can feel like discipline.

Divine discipline offers us a new perspective that can renew our hearts and minds. We may even see the value of the trial we just passed through. Divine discipline is given with the intention of helping to reshape us and remold us to become more of what God wants us to be. If we see it in that light, it can do our hearts good.

Today, discipline yourself in ways that serve to strengthen your heart and mind.

*Lord, help me to receive discipline in a more positive light,
as a way to become a better person in Your eyes. Amen.*

What Is World Peace?

I give you peace, the kind of peace that only I can give. It isn't like the peace that this world can give. So don't be worried or afraid.
JOHN 14:27 CEV

What kind of peace does Jesus give? It's the kind that passes all understanding, the kind that keeps you calm and content no matter what is playing out on the world stage. How can you tell if you have that kind of peace?

If you're looking for peace with your mind, your intellect, or anything but your spirit and your heart, you may not find it. Peace comes from knowing who you are, where you're headed, and from knowing the One who walks beside you and guides your steps every day.

The peace the world gives may not even be possible. Thankfully you have the peace that takes away fear and worry, the kind that allows your heart to be shaped by Jesus.

Lord, help me to find peace through Your Spirit each day. Amen.

What Is This Thing Called Love?

*"Let me give you a new command: Love one another.
In the same way I loved you, you love one another. This is
how everyone will recognize that you are my disciples—
when they see the love you have for each other."*

JOHN 13:34–35 MSG

God gave you a physical heart to help your body function well and to sustain the gift of life. He also gave you an emotional heart to help you see the world with love. He wants you to see every person around you with the eyes of compassion, mercy, and grace.

The thing is that love is the key to everything we do. It is the very reason Jesus came to earth. He is the embodiment of our understanding of the phrase "God is love." Wouldn't it be wonderful if we could show that kind of love to each person we meet today and every day? Spread a little love right where you are. You can be someone's valentine every day of the year.

*Lord, help us be Your examples of love and treat
everyone as a special valentine, no matter
what day of the year it is. Amen.*

Save the Planet

"I will also make you a light for the Gentiles,
that my salvation may reach to the ends of the earth."
ISAIAH 49:6 NIV

If you're not hiding your light under a bushel, but letting it shine over all those around you, then you have the right idea. You become a light to your family, your church, your community, your state, and in some way, to the world. Now the interesting aspect of the verse from Isaiah is that it says "I."

God tells Isaiah that He will make him a light to the nations so that the world can be saved. Seems like a small detail, but it is an important one. Just as the moon has no light of its own, but merely reflects the light of the sun, so you have no light of your own. You merely reflect the light of the Son. He makes you shine! He will help you act in the ways that bring His light to others. He will shape your thoughts, your words, and your deeds.

You're His moonbeam!

Lord, help me to reflect Your light in all that I do today.
Give me a heart that reflects You—always. Amen.

Discover Your Good Side

Your love must be real. Hate what is evil,
and hold on to what is good.

ROMANS 12:9 NCV

Sometimes, even when we agree with a cause, we decide that we cannot get involved, or we assume other people are already taking care of the problem and have it well in hand. Other times, we imagine we can't solve the troubles of the world because it's such an overwhelming task. That kind of thinking is certainly valid.

However, somewhere in your own sphere of influence, opportunity will knock and ask you to stand on the side of good. It will ask you to show others that you really do love them because you're willing to stand up for something. The old adage that "if you don't stand for something, you'll fall for anything" isn't totally off the mark. Stand up for love and discover more of what you can really do to be a champion for the good side!

Lord, thank You for the freedom to express ourselves
about things we believe in. Help me to stand with
others when You lead me to do so. Amen.

The Principle of Peter

*Peter fairly exploded with his good news: "It's God's own
truth, nothing could be plainer: God plays no favorites!
It makes no difference who you are or where you're
from—if you want God and are ready to do
as he says, the door is open."*
ACTS 10:34–35 MSG

We live in a culture that loves to put labels on everything. We label school-kids as gifted, special needs, or
any number of classifications. We label adults as company presidents, blue-collar workers, aggressive, or lazy.
We label our foods and we label our clothes and we label
our churches.

Chances are, taking away the labels would put a lot
of things back on neutral ground. Peter's description of
those who are acceptable to God reminds us that sometimes we get a little too caught up in the labels. God-
fearing people are everywhere. . .all over the world. God
has labeled those people as His.

As you go out into the world today, meet people
heart-first, extend the hand of fellowship and forget
about worrying about their title or position in life.

*Lord, help us to remember that You're not playing
favorites, for You created every one of us and gave
us all a way to be part of Your family. Amen.*

Goodness, What's Wrong?

In those days there was no king in Israel;
every man did what was right in his own eyes.
JUDGES 17:6 NASB

Many people appear to be living according to what they believe to be right in their own eyes, but living according to the "gospel of you" breaks down if you believe it's okay to steal a car from the driveway, kidnap a child, or steal someone's identity online. Some people live as though there was no king in Israel, that is, no Jesus, or no God of this universe.

How can you live with Jesus in your heart then? By believing that there is indeed a King who rules over you. You can seek Him and do all you can to spend your life on earth in ways that please Him, in ways that are right in His eyes. If you wonder if something you may do is right or wrong for you, consult with the One who still reigns. . . yesterday, today, and forever.

Lord, help me to live according to the commands of Jesus,
the King of my heart, and to step aside from those
things that would bring You sorrow. Amen.

What Did You Say?

*"You can be sure that on the Judgment Day
you will have to give account of every
useless word you have ever spoken."*
MATTHEW 12:36 GNT

This passage from Matthew is downright scary. It reminds us that God does not take our words lightly, that what we say matters. Are you ready to give an account of every useless word you've ever spoken? God have mercy!

Going forward, it might be good for all of us to take a little more notice of what we say and how we say it. The old phrase that you may have to eat those words, be forced to digest the things you once said, might not be too far from the truth. Let the words you speak today be sweet and refreshing!

Keep in mind that it's not just about your good words to others but the words others speak to you as well. Encourage kind words any way you can.

*Lord, help me to remember that everything I say to
lift another person up is meaningful. Let me
speak only words of love today. Amen.*

Tender Words

A soft answer turns away wrath,
but a harsh word stirs up anger.
PROVERBS 15:1 NKJV

What we say is so important to the well-being of others, and to the spirit within each of us, that we must be very conscious of our words, our tone, and our intentions any time we speak. We must remember to protect the hearts of others in our interactions. Today, let us recognize the amazing power of words and how we can offer them in kindness, gentleness, and a spirit of healing.

Francis de Sales said, "Nothing is so strong as gentleness, nothing so gentle as real strength." Let your words always be shared for the good of another. What you say really matters, so be sure to let your heart speak into any situation. Let your words always be full of grace and blessing.

Lord, in every conversation that I am part
of today, may Your Spirit prevail to bring
gentleness and self-control. Amen.

Thinking Clearly

So prepare your minds for action
and exercise self-control.
1 PETER 1:13 NLT

What you think is controlled by what you believe about yourself and about the world around you. What you believe is based on the actual center of your life, in other words on your faith in God as the Source of all things. What you believe is a matter of the heart, and from your heart you make important choices.

Your thoughts help you or hurt you as you respond to the world. You can pay more attention to your thoughts and beliefs. You can be clear with yourself and with others about what really motivates the things you say and do. You can do these things because of the grace of God within you.

When you lead with your heart, and follow in the footsteps of your Savior, everything feels more balanced, more blessed, and in control.

Lord, be in control of my thoughts and actions
today, so that each thought comes from
a heart focused on You. Amen.

Always Be Joyful

Always be joyful. Never stop praying.
Be thankful in all circumstances, for this is
God's will for you who belong to Christ Jesus.
1 THESSALONIANS 5:16–18 NLT

You may agree that you can find joy in simplicity. After all, it's the little things about the day that are often the highlights: a warm conversation with a friend, a favorite cup of hot chocolate, or even a great prayer time in the morning.

Joy is often a result of having a sense of well-being and self-respect. It is a divine attribute and a divine gift. One way to keep joyful is to honor your connection to Christ in everything you do. Seek His will for your life and you may find continual gifts of joy and a heart that overflows with His grace and goodness.

Keep on praying, keep on following, keep on being joyful, for that is your divine calling.

Lord, thank You for bringing Your Son, Jesus,
into the world to offer us an abundance
of joy so that our spirits thrive. Amen.

It's Time for a Hug!

For I hope to visit you soon and talk with
you face to face. Then our joy will be complete.
2 JOHN 12 NLT

Since connection and relationship are so important to us, we welcome friends into our homes, visit shut-ins who may need our help, or spend time with those in our church family. We have greater joy when we are aligned with people who understand us and who share the things that matter most to our hearts.

Your personal relationships are matters of the heart. Whenever you can, make plans to get together with people you love, make a few phone calls, or make a comment on Facebook so the people you love know they are often on your mind and always in your heart. A face-to-face hug is always the best, but a hug from the heart, reminding others you are still there, can change a drab day into a sparkling one.

Lord, remind me today how important my friends
are and how special my family is. Give us
a chance for more big hugs. Amen.

Let's Be Friends!

"I've told you these things for a purpose: that my joy might be your joy, and your joy wholly mature. This is my command: Love one another the way I loved you. This is the very best way to love. Put your life on the line for your friends. You are my friends when you do the things I command you. I'm no longer calling you servants because servants don't understand what their master is thinking and planning. No, I've named you friends because I've let you in on everything I've heard from the Father."

JOHN 15:11–15 MSG

As a friend of Jesus, you have every reason to rise with a smile on your face, say your prayers with gusto, and go about your day with the intention of feeling every bit of joy meant for you.

In fact, you become a joy ambassador. Everywhere you go, you share what you have. You think first of Jesus, then of others, and finally of yourself, and by definition lead a life of joy, or at least a day of joy. All that joy can't help attracting others and causing your friendships to grow.

A desire for friendship comes from a place deep within you and is lit by the Spirit Himself. It's your day to shine and to make friends with your whole heart!

Father, help me remember today that You have given me a light to share with the world around me. Amen.

So Grateful for God's Guidance

*I will bless the LORD who guides me; even at night my
heart instructs me. I know the LORD is always with me.
I will not be shaken, for he is right beside me.*

PSALM 16:7–8 NLT

God has been teaching us our whole lives and it feels
good to know that we're getting divine guidance. Think
about all the things you have learned so far. It's truly
amazing! Perhaps you even remember dreams that
helped to guide you, or moments you've shared in God's
presence that filled you with great confidence and joy.
As you go through this day, ask God what else He would
like your heart to know. What else you can do to grow
more compassionate and giving, more generous and loving. Share your heart with God and let Him mold you into
the person He knows you can be.

It is always right to give God thanks and praise for
what He has done in your life. Hug Him to your heart
everywhere you go today.

*Lord, let me be a child again in Your presence today.
Let me sit at Your feet and learn from You. Amen.*

Cheerfully Patient

God is the one who makes us patient and cheerful.
I pray that he will help you live at peace
with each other, as you follow Christ.

ROMANS 15:5 CEV

When you find yourself momentarily losing it over the little things that come at you during the day, it's time to stop everything and seek God's peace. After all, you can only be stretched just so thin before you start to lose a willingness to have good judgment or offer grace to those around you. Lots of things can steal your peace and only a little heart to heart with Jesus can really bring you back to joy.

Ask God to help you when your patience is simply maxed out. Bask in His presence until you are truly restored and refreshed to continue on with the day. He'll quiet your jangled nerves and give you more ways to be cheerfully patient. He'll make your heart glad once again.

Lord, help me to be an example of cheerful
patience in all that I do today. Amen.

He Knows Your Heart's Desire

*May he grant your heart's desires and make all your
plans succeed. May we shout for joy when we hear of
your victory and raise a victory banner in the name
of our God. May the LORD answer all your prayers.*

PSALM 20:4–5 NLT

God knows the desires of your heart. He put those
desires there. He wants you to become a person who
seeks His heart and then uses your heart in the ways that
you treat others. He sees you as someone who can bring
peace, comfort, and joy to those around you. When you
respond to the world with your heart, you are a child
after the heart of the Creator.

As you seek His direction for your life today, may you
discover that each step you take is one that is guided by
His hand and that all your plans are fulfilled with glad-
ness. May God be honored by all that you do today.

*Lord, guide me today to follow the desires of my heart
according to Your will and purpose for me. Help me
to see Your loving hand at work in my life. Amen.*

Wholehearted Waiting

Wait patiently for the LORD. Be brave and courageous.
Yes, wait patiently for the LORD.
PSALM 27:14 NLT

Having the heart to wait for something takes a fair amount of bravado. It means you have to stay positive, be upbeat, and keep busy while you wait. It means you have to trust that God is acting on your behalf even when you can't see or feel that anything is happening. Sometimes, it's in the waiting that you discover what is really important, what matters most to your heart and soul.

Today, pray for all the people you know who are waiting for something important in their lives. Pray that they too will be brave and courageous. Pray that God will reveal to their waiting hearts the blessings of what will yet come.

Lord, help me to value the time that passes while
I'm waiting for good to come. Help me to
trust You with my whole heart. Amen.

A Day of Fresh Mercy

The faithful love of the LORD never ends!
His mercies never cease. Great is his faithfulness;
his mercies begin afresh each morning.
LAMENTATIONS 3:22–23 NLT

You can pick a new bunch of mercies like grapes from a vine because you are indeed part of the real Vine. You can draw near to Him and allow Him to anoint your day, your family, and your work so that you can be at peace. You can start again with a clean slate.

This is not a small promise! If we look at our yesterdays and those things that we've done to mess up God's perfect plans for our lives, we might get downhearted and lose sight of the possibilities before us. We might even forget that God can do anything, including taking a big eraser and giving us a fresh start.

Let your heart rejoice and do a happy dance as you live today in the abundance of God's grace and mercy!

Lord, I am in awe of Your tender mercies,
and I'm grateful each day that I can
trust in them again. Amen.

Sometimes Your Heart Hurts

I am exhausted and completely crushed.
My groans come from an anguished heart.
PSALM 38:8 NLT

Sometimes the light goes out and you don't know which way to turn or what the clear path might be that is best for you or someone you love. You would like to help, but nothing you've done makes a difference. Some people turn to friends, drugs, or alcohol. You turn to God.

Today, you may not have a situation that hurts, but you may know someone else who does. Remind them, if you can, that they are not alone. Remind them of the Source of light and healing. As you do so, be God's hands and heart for that person. Your efforts will cause your own spirits to rise.

God sees what you do and will be proud of the way you share your heart even during difficult times with those around you. Rest in His love and healing power today. He knows what you need.

Lord, help me to rest in Your care and offer hope
to others when life causes them pain. Amen.

A Compassionate Heart

*But when He saw the multitudes, He was moved
with compassion for them, because they were weary
and scattered, like sheep having no shepherd.*
MATTHEW 9:36 NKJV

When we're weary, it's hard to make good decisions. It's hard to know where to turn or how to find meaningful solutions to our problems. Jesus had compassion on people because He could see that they were lost. They were overwhelmed by life and simply didn't have any sense that things could change.

You have a compassionate heart every time you pay attention to the needs of others. You see their needs and you want more than anything to help them. God wants to equip you to be part of their solution.

Today, seek God's help as you step into the world. Ask Him to draw near to you, providing what you need from His strength and love to make a difference in the lives of others. The blessings you share will fall back on you a hundredfold.

*Lord, help us to come to You for strength
and renewal as our Good Shepherd. Amen.*

Be Kind, Please!

Be kind to each other.
EPHESIANS 4:32 NLT

Think about how you feel when a total stranger offers you a helping hand. Maybe you needed a jumper cable to start your car or you were feeling frenzied by all you needed to accomplish in a day, and someone reached out and helped you without even needing to be asked. Maybe you simply needed a warm smile to refresh your spirits.

Today, if you can think of anyone who needs a tender touch of kindness, something you can provide in a generous dose, then send it their way. Be the ambassador of kindness wherever you go. Kindness won't cost you a thing, but it will enrich your life enormously and your heart will grow three times its size and bring you joy.

Lord, I do try to be kind to those around me, but help me today to be especially aware of those that might not receive enough of the milk of human kindness. Amen.

Just a Gentle Word

Gentle words cause life and health.
PROVERBS 15:4 TLB

Think of the kindest person you know; the one who gives compliments from the heart. They warm your heart and make you glad to be in their presence. They have a way of doing good deeds without even noticing the great help they are to others. They just know what to say to make you smile. They make you feel confident, loved, and cared about.

Being a person of kind words is a gift. Most of us try to be kind in general, but the person who came to mind in the paragraph above would be labeled as truly kind and be viewed in a different category. Maybe there's room for more of us to join them. Let's use gentle words all day, making heartfelt and affirming compliments to those around us. It will cause our hearts to be glad.

Lord, remind me that You can work within me to help me share more gifts of kindness with others. Amen.

Writing a Little Love Note

*Beautiful words stir my heart. I will recite a lovely
poem about the king, for my tongue is
like the pen of a skillful poet.*
PSALM 45:1 NLT

♥

Imagine today that your heart overflows with joy about
someone dear. You could send them a quick text and
suggest that you're thinking of them, but maybe seeing
your handwriting on some nice stationery will be even
more important—a gift they can keep and read over and
over again.

God sent us His love letter in the form of the Bible,
written down so that every day we can go back and read
some of it; or reread portions that hold the most meaning
for us. This is your day to write a little love note to someone you love. Take the time to share your heart and your
handwriting, and add to the joy of the whole experience.

*Lord, thank You for inspiring my thoughts to send a note
or a letter to someone special today. I pray that I will
try more often to make my communication with the
people who are dear to me even more personal
by writing in my own hand. Amen.*

Joy Is an Action Word

Ask and you will receive,
and your joy will be complete.
JOHN 16:24 NIV

It's true that we can't do everything, but we can do something. We can pick one cause, one charity, one family, one friend, one something that will become the object of our help and our kindness. We can answer the call of our own hearts to contribute to being a solution for someone else's concerns.

Ask God to guide you today to where He most wants you to share your gifts, your talents, and your kindness. You can offer a bit of hope by a generous gesture, or suggest a new path of possibility for someone to consider. God will use your smallest effort so it becomes someone else's greatest good.

Deepen my desire to reach out in a new direction to offer
Your joy to others, Lord. Help me to always be willing
to share what I can as a matter of heart. Amen.

Ambassadors Forever

We are Christ's ambassadors;
God is making his appeal through us.
2 CORINTHIANS 5:20 NLT

As someone with the gift of God's Spirit, you serve as an ambassador for Christ. As an ambassador of the heart, you open the way for greater understanding, conversation, and opportunity for those around you. You help bridge the gap about things they may misunderstand about God, themselves, or others. You are the messenger to bring them hope, and you deliver your message for their sake even more than for your own.

When you signed up to be a Christian, you took this role for life. Whatever you do from here reflects God's heart working within you. It is through your heart and hands that many others will be blessed. May God bless you with opportunities to shine for Him and keep you always in His favor.

Lord, You always have work for me to do, and I thank You.
Help me to do it with Your heart and Your Spirit. Amen.

Stolen Peace

Don't worry about anything; instead, pray about everything. Tell God what you need, and thank him for all he has done. Then you will experience God's peace, which exceeds anything we can understand.

PHILIPPIANS 4:6–7 NLT

How much does it cost you to worry? We have an intellectual understanding that worry never helps, but for some reason, it's nearly the first thing we do when things are not going our way.

At the very least, worry is expensive. It can bring poor health to your body and your mind. It can require medication to get you through the challenges it manufactures in your head, the stories that simply won't stop spinning there.

Today, stop worrying. It won't be easy, but you have other choices. You can pray about everything and put your anxieties in God's hand. You can put the burdens down and place your troubles at the foot of the cross. If you do, God's promise is that you can experience His peace and give your heart and mind a rest.

Lord, I surrender my worries to You and place them at the cross. Amen.

A Heart-Shaped Life that Frees!

Every way of a man is right in his own eyes,
but the LORD weighs the hearts.
PROVERBS 21:2 NKJV

♥

God is always seeking our hearts. He weighs what we do by the intention of our hearts. When you give with a generous and loving heart, it's very different than when you give, even the same amount of time, money, or effort, with a heart that simply feels obligated. Your heart is either shaped by God's desire for you to draw closer to Him and understand His ways, or it is shaped by the world, which has no guidance at all.

Whatever is right for you, pray that God will direct your steps so much that you will know exactly what He has in mind. Pray that He will see your generous and loving intentions and bless the direction you take. This is the joy of a heart-shaped life; one that frees you to be exactly who you are in the eyes of your Creator.

Lord, help me to stay so close to You that
all I do has Your stamp on it. Amen.

Separating the Good from the Bad

A good tree can't produce bad fruit, and a bad tree can't produce good fruit. . . . Yes, just as you can identify a tree by its fruit, so you can identify people by their actions.

MATTHEW 7:18, 20 NLT

It isn't always easy to tell the good people from the bad ones. In our culture, we're often drawn to the beautiful people because we make the assumption that they would just naturally be good. The problem is that we're wrong a good share of the time.

At some point, we discover that beauty and goodness do not necessarily go hand in hand. Perhaps we just don't understand beauty. If we understood God's definitions of beauty a bit more clearly, we would see that the good person is always a beautiful person. Goodness and beauty do go together when they emanate from the Spirit of God.

Whatever your definition of beauty might be, remember that God searches for beauty from the inside out. You can too. Being good has nothing to do with your wardrobe or your wallet. It has everything to do with your heart.

Lord, help me to seek what is beautiful in others based on their love for You and their love for other people. Shape my heart to be a better person in Your eyes. Amen.

Sometimes, It's Not about You

No one should seek their own good,
but the good of others.
1 CORINTHIANS 10:24 NIV

For your own good, let go of thinking about yourself and start to think about others. If you step out of your world for a few minutes and reach out to help someone else, you might discover that things look different than they did before. Lending a helping hand takes away your focus on your own troubles and helps you begin to feel better. Helping others is a sure cure for what ails you.

Giving your heart and your help to those outside your four walls may not take away the things that led you to wanting to curl up in a blanket, but you'll recognize that it's not all about you and that you're not alone. There's a world out there and everyone needs a little help sometimes. Seek the good of others and God will bless you tenfold.

Lord, help me remember that I'm not the only one
with problems to solve. Help me do what I can for
others, regardless of my own situation. Amen.

Patience with Yourself and Others

Be completely humble and gentle; be patient,
bearing with one another in love.
EPHESIANS 4:2 NIV

♥

Just be patient! You might bear the waiting in your head, but it's a little harder to do when the issue is a matter of the heart. When you're waiting for someone you care about to find a better life path, to trust God more, or to see that they are losing ground, then it's harder to wait. God gave you a heart that anticipates and grows excited with new ideas and opportunities. It rejoices when you see His hand at work in your life and in the lives of others. It even does some flip-flops of gratitude when things come together.

Your heart is not always practical and patient though. The more you recognize how often you have to be patient with others, the more you recognize the same principles apply to you. Be humble and gentle today, bearing with others and trusting in God to lead you. It will be worth any waiting you have to do.

Lord, help me to be more of what You would have
me be and wait with a humble and loving
heart when I'm called to do so. Amen.

Love Is at the Heart of Everything

For this very reason, make every effort to add to your faith goodness; and to goodness, knowledge; and to knowledge, self-control; and to self-control, perseverance; and to perseverance, godliness; and to godliness, mutual affection; and to mutual affection, love.

2 PETER 1:5–7 NIV

Adding goodness and self-control to your life always means you'll enjoy a little more of the good stuff life has to offer. After all, the more you give, share, and offer to others in the right spirit, the more will come back to you. Brotherly and sisterly kindness and love will reward you.

As someone living a heart-shaped life, God looks to you to lead the way. He wants you to shine your light on His people who have not yet seen Him clearly and offer to help them do so. He wants you to give in ways that you may not have thought possible simply because of your love for Him. He knows you. He knows you have a lot to give, and He knows that love is at the heart of everything you do.

Lord, whatever I do today, help me to do it with Your amazing love. Amen.

The Bigness of God

This is what the LORD says—your Redeemer and Creator:
"I am the LORD, who made all things. I alone stretched out
the heavens. Who was with me when I made the earth?"
ISAIAH 44:24 NLT

When you leave God in charge of everything, you set your priorities in order. You remind yourself that nothing exists because of you, but everything exists because of Him. You give up your own need to be in control, and you even stop asking "why." You just let the divine greatness of God be the master of all things, including you. Let God be God and let Him be even bigger in your life.

One of the ways you know you're growing more "heart-shaped" is when you recognize that God is everything and that nothing else truly makes a difference. God working within you makes the whole difference to your life and what you share by His grace with others. He gave you a big heart because He is a big God!

Lord, You're big enough to handle everything.
Thank You for allowing me to help You where I can,
sharing in the joy of working with my Father. Amen.

Happy Circumstances!

Good planning and hard work lead to prosperity.
PROVERBS 21:5 NLT

Part of our faithfulness to God is about not giving excuses when things don't go the way we hope they will. God is always available to help us create "happy circumstances" that will benefit our hearts and minds. He wants us to include Him in the planning and to be faithful in the asking.

If you don't see what you want for your life today, perhaps your first step in the planning is not to see what you can do, not to rely on your own strength, but to seek God's heart for the opportunity you have in mind. He'll be able to help you move toward your goal with joy. He'll shape your heart to seek Him first so you can discover His will for your life.

Lord, let me work with You to create
the best circumstances for my life.
My heart rejoices in You! Amen.

The Commandment to Love

*Jesus said, "'Love the Lord your God with all your passion
and prayer and intelligence.' This is the most important
[of God's commands], the first on any list."*
MATTHEW 22:37-38 MSG

When love commands you to seek God, you have lots of
ways to do so. Look at the things that make your heart
sing, give you renewed energy, and bring your spirit to
life. When that feeling permeates your soul, you are better
able to demonstrate your love for God.

You can honor God with your prayers. Take everything to Him. Put your sorrows and concerns and "what-ifs" at His feet. Put your joys, your excitement, and your hopes in His arms and embrace His love.

You can honor God with your intelligence. Give Him everything that goes on in your heart and mind. Surrender your goals and your ambitions and your dreams and trust Him to return to you those things that are truly yours.

Renew your commitment to love God and enjoy the pleasure of His company in even greater measure today.

*Dear God, help me to love You as You deserve to be
loved. I surrender my passion, my heart, my mind,
and my spirit to Your care and keeping. Amen.*

Love One Another

*"But there is a second [command of God] to set
alongside it: 'Love others as well as you love yourself.' "*
MATTHEW 22:39 MSG

A command to love others as we love ourselves puts some of us in jeopardy. In part, it's because we've bought into the negative things others have said about us, or we have decided we're not very lovable. So we simply don't know how to love ourselves, and by extension, we're not good at loving others either. In fact, we're not really sure what this command of Jesus really means.

If you've forgotten how to love yourself, take a moment and consider creating ways that might renew your understanding. Give yourself a gift of honoring YOU. Take note of each time you do, say, or understand something about yourself that allows you to see your heart the way God sees you. He loves you, imperfections and all. He doesn't love you for what you aren't. He loves you for what you are!

*Lord, I know I'm pretty stingy with myself.
Help me to understand what it means
to have genuine self-love. Amen.*

Have No Fear

"All who listen to me will live in peace,
untroubled by fear of harm."
PROVERBS 1:33 NLT

It's not easy to keep peace within your soul these days. Five minutes of watching the news or reading the paper and you feel anxious.

You may not have choices about the forces of nature, or even about people who would continually try to wrap you in blankets of fear, but you do have choices about how long you allow your mind to dwell on those things. You can make yourself ill with the thinking, or you can give your fears to God. He will listen!

God does not want you to live in fear. He wants you to know that He is bigger than all of these issues. He sees you right where you are. He wants you to lean on Him for protection and strength. Ask Him to keep you safe and help you maintain peace in your heart. His peace is yours for the asking.

Father, please protect me, and those I love, and keep us
safe from harm. Help us to count on You, no matter
what we see in the news of the day. Amen.

Being the Gatekeeper

*I would rather be a gatekeeper in the house of my
God than live the good life in the homes of the
wicked. For the LORD God is our sun and our
shield. He gives us grace and glory.*

PSALM 84:10–11 NLT

For a person of faith, "the good life" is often about service to God. That service means sharing in His presence and His goodness, His light and His protection every day. As one of God's gatekeepers, it's important for you to determine exactly where you want to stand. You want to open the door so that others can also stand. It's your heart that determines the "good life" and your heart that seeks God's light and protection.

Being a loving servant, tending the gate, and welcoming those around you into God's presence can be the calling of your life. As you keep the gate open, honor God by bringing others closer to His side.

*Lord, the gates to temptation are everywhere and I know
they do not lead me closer to You. Help me to be
a more vigilant gatekeeper. Amen.*

Encourage One Another

All of you should be of one mind. Sympathize with
each other. Love each other as brothers and sisters.
Be tenderhearted, and keep a humble attitude.
1 PETER 3:8 NLT

You can hardly read the daily paper of any city in the country without feeling compassion for people all over the globe. Your heart suffers with those who have undergone severe losses because of illness or natural disasters. You have a great desire to volunteer your time to help build a house with Habitat for Humanity or visit a shut-in and offer a word of encouragement. When you respond in a way that does your heart good, an interesting thing happens. You're given an instant gift. That gift is peace, and an even bigger heart.

May God continue to work with you, reminding you that you are His hands and feet in a world that is desperately in need of hope and tenderhearted encouragement.

Dear Lord, help me to reach out with genuine sympathy to
those in need around me. Remind me that anything
I have comes to me from Your goodness
and Your grace. Amen.

A Contented Heart

I have learned, in whatsoever state I am,
therewith to be content.

PHILIPPIANS 4:11 KJV

Restless hearts are not contented ones. They search everywhere for a way to calm their stretched nerves and quiet their spirits. They look for antidotes in pharmacies or liquor bottles, hoping for relief from whatever ails their hearts and minds. They exercise until their bodies are too tired to think anymore, or so they'll have enough stamina to carry the load again tomorrow.

You can have a contented heart. You can be content in whatever circumstances you have and be at peace with yourself. You can because your Father in heaven wants you to be at peace, and He gave you the gift of His peace through the Holy Spirit. Embrace Him. Open the gift of peace and don't leave home without it. Go on your way with a truly contented heart today.

Lord, it is not easy for me to find peace in the world,
in my home, and in my heart. Quiet my heart,
and help me today to rest in You. Amen.

Destiny Awaits!

When a potter makes jars out of clay, doesn't he have a right to use the same lump of clay to make one jar for decoration and another to throw garbage into?

ROMANS 9:21 NLT

It's not always easy to remember that you are not the Potter, but simply the clay. As the clay, you can be used by God in any way He chooses for the good of His whole human family. He clearly needs each of us to do different things to help usher in the Kingdom.

Your destiny is in His hands. If you give Him the right to mold you and hold you close, you'll discover that He has something beautiful in mind for you to become. He delights in you simply because you allow Him to utilize your skills and talents and ideas in whatever way pleases Him. He loves your willingness to give Him your whole heart, surrendering to His design for your life. Your future then is to be more beautiful in whatever use He has for your life.

Lord, help me to become all that You intended me to become by the works of Your hand. Let me be a labor of love, and a joy to Your Spirit. Amen.

Producing the Good Fruit

*"A good tree can't produce bad fruit,
and a bad tree can't produce good fruit."*
LUKE 6:43 NLT

The Bible often makes the point that who and what we are has a lot to do with what goes on in the heart. We say that someone is good-hearted when they do kind deeds for others, or when they give selflessly to the well-being of those around them. Their work is a direct result of what they believe. In fact, everything they do is closely tied to the discipline of their hearts. You recognize those people by the fruit of their labors.

You often do good deeds. You give from the heart to those in need and to the people in your family. Challenge yourself today to produce even more of the great fruit. See if there is one person in your sphere of influence you may have overlooked. Keep growing, keep producing good fruit, and keep sharing your heart with others.

*Lord, remind me of those people I have
overlooked and who need my help,
and give me an opportunity to
plant new seeds of love. Amen.*

Working for Peace

You may not be a speaker, a writer, or a group leader, but you can still contribute to the peace in the world. How? You can be the keeper of peace in your own home or in your workplace. You can be the voice of reason when conflict arises. You can pray for the good of everyone you know so that their lives have greater peace. You can be a force for good simply by doing those things. You can remind people that they are connected—neighbor to neighbor and heart to heart.

Open the door for peace in your heart, your home, and your community. You can shape the way people see each other, restore a sense of calm, and honor each one as a unique child of God.

*Lord, help me offer Your peace to all those I meet,
remembering that each person is known by
You, and each one is loved. Amen.*

Be the Light

"You are the light of the world—like a city on a hilltop that cannot be hidden. No one lights a lamp and then puts it under a basket. Instead, a lamp is placed on a stand, where it gives light to everyone in the house."

MATTHEW 5:14–15 NLT

When you live a heart-shaped life, you discover that everything you do and say is affected by the Spirit of God living within you. You can be the light in many wonderful ways. Every time you offer a smile and a kind word to someone, you're the light. Every time you have compassion on your neighbor or even a stranger, you're the light. Every time you do something as the hands and feet of Christ, you're the light. In fact, unless you're sound asleep, you're actively engaged in being a shining star.

Your prayers are like the stars in heaven. They sparkle, shine, and illuminate the way for all those you offer up to God. You bring their needs to light and focus attention on them. Every time you pray, the light shines.

Lord, help me to shine Your light as brightly as I can today. Let me be the light of kindness, of friendship, and of compassion every chance I get. Amen.

Be Cheerful All the Time!

Be cheerful no matter what; pray all the time;
thank God no matter what happens. This is the way
God wants you who belong to Christ Jesus to live.
1 THESSALONIANS 5:16-18 MSG

Whatever happens in your everyday life, you are a child of God, a follower of Jesus, and that means you have good reason to be cheerful. Your situation may seem less than what you'd hope for, but if you keep your heart connected to your Savior, and stay focused on Him, then you have reason for joy.

You may not be happy about each detail of your life, but you can always be happy in Jesus. It may be harder to remember this some days when things are not going well, but start with today and trust God with your heart, soul, and mind. It could make all the difference. You might even find yourself smiling.

Lord, help me to find my joy in You no matter what
is going on in my life. Help me to surrender the
details of living on earth and embrace
the joy of living in Jesus. Amen.

Love Forgives

Hatred stirs up trouble, but love forgives all wrongs.
PROVERBS 10:12 NCV

Saying I'm sorry can be difficult. Meaning it deep within the heart can be even more challenging. We can't say we're sorry and then remind the person of the wrong deed every time we get a chance. How would we feel if God did that to us? He puts our sins far from Him and remembers them no more. That's what a forgiving heart does. That's what He wants us to do too. We haven't forgiven what we truly haven't forgotten.

Love forgives all wrongs. Sometimes love forgives even without apologies. Love puts all wrongs at the cross of Christ and leaves them there.

That's loving and forgiving at its best. Go on, you can do it.

Lord, let me learn to be truly forgiving out of love for You.
Help me to surrender any need to forgive or be forgiven
to You and move on in Your grace and mercy. Amen.

Dare to Dream. . .Dare to Ask!

*You can ask for anything in my name, and I will
do it, so that the Son can bring glory to the Father.
Yes, ask me for anything in my name, and I will do it!*
JOHN 14:13–14 NLT

What do you dream and hope for and fear all at the same time? It is important to be a lover of dreams for that is what fills the heart with joy and expectation. It is important to be a lover of prayer for the same reason. Prayer puts a foundation under your dreams and lifts them to a place of fulfillment and opportunity. Prayer puts your dreams in direct alignment with God. Ask Him to line your heart up with the dreams He's given you so that you can work together to create the vision.

Sometimes we dream, sometimes we pray, but often we forget to put our dreams in the Creator's hands so He can help us manifest them according to His will and purpose for us. Ask! Ask for your heart's desires in Jesus' name!

*Lord, help me to embrace the ways You shape
the direction of my life, and help me to seek
Your wisdom in all that I do. Amen.*

Wealth or Riches?

*Command those who are rich with things of this world
not to be proud. Tell them to hope in God, not in their
uncertain riches. God richly gives us everything to enjoy.
Tell the rich people to do good, to be rich in doing
good deeds, to be generous and ready to share.*
1 TIMOTHY 6:17–18 NCV

♥

In God's sight, there's a big difference between wealthy people and rich people. Wealthy people have accumulated more toys and more of this world's goods. Rich people have accumulated more authentic friendships and relationships because of the ways they treat others. Wealthy people and rich people can both be generous and do great deeds with loving hearts. Heart-rich people are always the first to lend a hand when a crisis happens. The difference is not about money.

We can be rich beyond our wildest dreams, and that has nothing to do with the size of our bank accounts. It has to do with the size of our spirits and our hearts.

Regardless of your income level, you can be rich any time you choose to be. God will multiply your good deeds with His grace and favor.

*Lord, open my heart to new experiences, help me to
give generously wherever I can, and cause me to
pray continually for those in need. Amen.*

A Grateful Heart

Devote yourselves to prayer,
being watchful and thankful.
COLOSSIANS 4:2 NIV

One of the ways you might recognize that your heart is being shaped by God's hand is when you find yourself simply being more grateful for everything. You take a walk on a bright sunny day and feel your heart swell up with the beauty that surrounds you. You enjoy a visit with a good friend and walk away from the experience ready to praise God for His gift of giving you a friend like that. Wherever you go, you see His marvelous handiwork and you know that He is in control.

A thankful heart is a loving heart. It is a heart that knows that human beings exist, move, and breathe because of all that God has done. It is a heart that understands that it can never truly give God enough praise for this incredible home called earth.

Lord, thank You for the blessings You have given
to my life. I praise You for Your infinite
and unconditional love. Amen.

Soul Searching

"Search all of history, from the time God created people on the earth until now, and search from one end of the heavens to the other. Has anything as great as this ever been seen or heard before?"

DEUTERONOMY 4:32 NLT

When you seek God with your whole heart, He can be found. He is not hiding from you. He is not offended by you. He is not waiting to judge you. He is only waiting to have a relationship with you. He wants to share His heart with you and have you share yours. He wants to be your friend and your constant companion. He knows you already, and nothing would give Him more joy than to have you know Him in return.

Open your heart to God every day. Give Him a part of you that you've withheld; seek His face and His forgiveness. He'll bless your life a thousand-fold and give you the desires of your heart. Keep discovering the mystery, the passion, and the joy that comes from knowing God and of walking with Him in steadfast love.

Lord, thank You for lifting my heart by Your grace and helping me to discover new joys in You and in the blessings my soul receives anew each time I draw close to You again. Amen.

A Little Bit of Heaven

Let heaven and earth praise him,
the seas and all that move in them.
PSALM 69:34 NIV

When you live life heart-first, everything matters to you. Everything inspires your imagination to determine what you can do for the good of others.

Whatever creates a touch of heaven in your life is a gentle reminder of the love God has for you and the joy He wants you to have for yourself and to share with others. Your faith brings you into alignment with His will, and your trust in Him makes moments of joy come around more often. You have the opportunity any time you please to bring a little bit of heaven into the lives of those you love.

Stop for a moment and offer up your heartfelt thanks and praise, for He brings heaven to your soul.

Lord, thank You for blessing me with so many wonderful
moments to enjoy. Thank You for quiet times and
fun times with family and friends. Amen.

A Few Good Deeds

*Just as a person's body that does not have a spirit
is dead, so faith that does nothing is dead!*

JAMES 2:26 NCV

Whenever we have a passion for something, we want to live it, breathe it, and touch it as often as possible. We think about it most of the time, we learn more about it every chance we get, and we try to perfect our response to it. When your spirits are low though, you run out of energy and you can't feel the passion that lives within you.

What makes your passion come alive again? It's simple. It's a matter of doing something special for someone else, getting closely connected to the Spirit of the One who made you, and recognizing the gifts of the world around you. In Him is life, and that life is yours any time you call His name!

*Lord, help me to connect to You today in ways that
revitalize my spirit and renew my energy and
strength in You. Let me share my love
for You with those I meet. Amen.*

Cleaning Up Your Heart

Create in me a pure heart, O God,
and renew a steadfast spirit within me.
PSALM 51:10 NIV

Most of us need to do some clean-up work inside our minds and hearts now and then. We need to go in and vacuum out the spiderwebs of doubt or unbelief that manage to build little nests in our heads. We need to toss out a few old ideas that don't serve us very well and freshen up with the insights God has given us in more recent months. We need to be sure that our hearts are in the right place, that place that allows us to love God with our whole hearts, minds, and spirits.

Today, take a little dusting and cleaning time. Let go of things that hold you back from loving as much as you know you can and make room for more of God's Spirit to live within you.

Lord, help me get rid of those thoughts and ideas that
are not serving me or You today and replace them
with Your gentle Spirit of love. Amen.

Seize the Day!

Seize life! Eat bread with gusto, drink wine with a robust heart. Oh yes—God takes pleasure in your pleasure! Dress festively every morning. Don't skimp on colors and scarves. Relish life with the spouse you love each and every day of your precarious life. Each day is God's gift.

ECCLESIASTES 9:7 MSG

The teacher of Ecclesiastes had all the same issues you and I may have. He had to face the realities of life as he knew it and keep going. He had to keep trusting in God's love, mercy, and grace. Yet, he came away from all of that reminding us that each day is God's gift and each day we need to dress with joy and challenge the world with a robust heart. We need to and we can because God is right there watching over each breath we take.

When you live a life that is heart-shaped, it means you're so connected to God's desires for you that even the mundane things take on a sense of calling and offer personal reward. Go for the joy today in all you do!

Lord, I know You meant for me to enjoy life and to live it in a way that makes it all worthwhile. Bless me today, and help me seize the day with gusto! Amen.

Honor and Service

"So fear the LORD and serve him wholeheartedly."
JOSHUA 24:14 NLT

When Jesus commanded us to love God with our whole heart, He meant that we should do so with every breath, every opportunity, every service we might render. He meant that we should be committed to living with all the energy, gusto, and goodness that we could muster.

We live wholeheartedly because we want to honor Him in every possible way. Look at the things you're doing today. See if you can discover the moments that you're truly aware of serving God with great energy and enthusiasm, rather than simply doing a mindless task with no thought of purpose or no particular joy.

Awaken your spirit to the gift of serving with a heart of joy. It'll make your whole day go better. . .and your heart will desire to serve with abundance and love.

Lord, whether I'm reading a book or going to a job,
let me do it with the joy of knowing that anything
I do is part of my commitment to You. Amen.

A Kindly Word

Timely advice is lovely,
like golden apples in a silver basket.
PROVERBS 25:11 NLT

We shy away from sharing our hearts sometimes when it comes to giving advice to our friends. Why? We build up all kinds of reasons. We tell ourselves it's not our business, we shouldn't get involved, or they have a right to do what they want.

This proverb is a beautiful reminder that sometimes the most loving thing we can do is offer our advice. If we offer it in kindness, with a heart for good, with the intention that our thoughts may be helpful to the one we're sharing our thoughts with, then it is the right thing. Then, we have put beautiful golden apples in a silver basket.

Sometimes the Spirit Himself is prompting you to offer a helpful message. Be prayerful. Be kind. Lovingly share your heart with others and your advice will bear fruit.

Lord, help me know the difference between sharing
a self-motivated opinion and giving loving advice.
Help me to listen for Your direction in all
my conversations today. Amen.

Fix Your Thoughts

Fix your thoughts on what is true, and honorable,
and right, and pure, and lovely, and admirable.
Think about things that are excellent
and worthy of praise.
PHILIPPIANS 4:8 NLT

You have many things in your life that are true, and honorable, and right. The work of your hands or the relationships you share with your family may well come to mind. Or think about things that are lovely and admirable. Perhaps now you can smile at the thoughts of people in your life who easily express love and kindness.

Give yourself a chance right now to feel the joy of knowing you are a child of God and live as a child of God. Fix your thoughts on things above, and things on earth will feel more glorious. Go on! Put a flower in your lapel and remind yourself that every good gift comes from above, and your Father wants you to receive His gifts with joy. Think about all the excellent things He has done, and give Him praise.

Father, help me remember that You have generously
lavished me with gifts of love and joy. Amen.

When You Can't See Clearly

But we live by faith, not by what we see.
2 CORINTHIANS 5:7 CEV

When you're walking in the dark, remember that even though you can't see clearly, you can still hear clearly. You can listen for God's voice and seek His direction. If you stay attuned to His voice, you'll break through to the light again before you know it.

We sometimes say that people have blind faith. There is no such thing. Faith always lets in the light, and it always knows the right direction. It moves closer to God with each step. Faith knows that it follows after the heart of God. It dispels the darkness and lives in the light.

Helen Keller said, "If the blind put their hand in God's, they find their way more surely than those who see but have not faith or purpose." Continue in your faith and fulfill your life purpose.

---

*Lord, I am blinded sometimes by the trappings
of the world. I set my faith aside and try too hard
to trust my intellect. Help me walk closer
to You, even in the dark. Amen.*

Lifting Weights

*But without faith no one can please God. We must
believe that God is real and that he rewards
everyone who searches for him.*
HEBREWS 11:6 CEV

Most of us want to stay healthy. We watch our diet, try
to avoid too many desserts and too many visits to our
favorite fast-food chain, and we work out.

Faith is important for good health as well. It lifts you
up, strengthens you, and gives you a greater opportunity
to enjoy life. Your faith shouldn't be something you carry
around though; it should be something that carries you.
It should help you exercise all your connections to God
in very real ways. It will strengthen your spirit.

If you want to lift weights at the gym, go ahead. If you
want to lift weights off your life, go to God. He'll help you
lift your burdens. All you have to do is believe He's there.

*Lord, I raise my hands to You and invite You in today
to lift my burdens and help me enjoy all the good
things You want me to discover. Amen.*

Family Ties

God sets the lonely in families.
PSALM 68:6 NIV

The globe continues to shrink, and we have all become more familiar with family life on other continents and within other cultures. We're becoming increasingly aware that we are truly much more alike than we are different from our neighbors. We all seek love, approval, and joy within our families. When we can't find those things there, we move beyond them and create new "families" out of those closest to us.

As children of God, we all have the same Father, and in a very real sense we're all related. We're family! We can learn to love one another and find common joys and gifts to share, or we can become estranged and dysfunctional, forgetting that we're of royal blood.

As you celebrate with your family this summer, remember that your kinship is deeper than simply sharing some common last names. You share the same Father.

---

*Lord, help me to appreciate and love the family
You have given me, honoring Your name
in all my relationships there. Amen.*

Rivers of Hope

*I pray that God, the source of hope, will fill you
completely with joy and peace because you trust in
him. Then you will overflow with confident hope
through the power of the Holy Spirit.*

ROMANS 15:13 NLT

Don't you love sitting by a peaceful riverbank on a warm,
sunny day? Maybe there are just a few light clouds in the
sky and you can close your eyes and hear the crickets
chirping and the fish jumping. You're totally at peace.

Is anything keeping you from flowing over with peace
even when you're not on the riverbank? Is your hope
choked by weeds and your joy simply suffocating under
layers upon layers of life's problems? Then sit back, close
your eyes, and take five minutes to renew your spirit and
walk along the riverbank. God is waiting there to refresh
you and give you a sense of peace and power that can
only come through the Holy Spirit.

It's your right as a child of God to experience rivers
of peace and splashes of deep joy. All you have to do is
rest quietly by the Source of Living Water.

*Lord, help me today to rest in Your fountains of
joy. Remind me that You are with me always,
and grant me Your peace. Amen.*

From Gloom to Bloom

*Some people brought to him [Jesus] a paralyzed man on
a mat. Seeing their faith, Jesus said to the paralyzed man,
"Be encouraged, my child! Your sins are forgiven."*
MATTHEW 9:2 NLT

Friends played a big role in the life of the paralyzed man.
They literally brought him to Jesus, mat and all. They knew
in their hearts that Jesus could heal him and that their
friend would be able to walk again. Sometimes it takes
that kind of faith, the kind that comes from those around
you believing for you until you can walk on your own.

Whatever is keeping you down today, the Lord
says, "Be encouraged, my child! Your sins are forgiven."
You are free now to celebrate, move around, jump up
and down, and rejoice in the grace of God because the
clouds are moving. The sun is coming out again, and it's
time for you to bloom.

*Lord, I thank You for the friends who hold me up in prayer
and keep me in front of Your throne. I thank You for
blessing me and bringing me great joy. Amen.*

Make the World Brighter

*"When you put on a luncheon or a banquet," he said,
"don't invite your friends, brothers, relatives, and rich
neighbors. For they will invite you back, and that will
be your only reward. Instead, invite the poor, the crippled,
the lame, and the blind. Then at the resurrection of
the righteous, God will reward you for inviting
those who could not repay you."*
LUKE 14:12–14 NLT

You are a part of God's way for making the world a better place. You may do it by inviting the lost and the lame to sit at your table, or you might feed the hungry through your favorite charity group. Whatever you prefer to do, you do it with a heart of grace and kindness! You do it because you know that you can make a difference! God will always reward you for helping those who could not repay you.

In fact, He already has! Give Him thanks and praise that you are in a position even now to make the world a little bit brighter and better.

*Lord, sometimes I take for granted the warm bed
I sleep in and the nutritious meal I eat at dinnertime.
You lavish so much on me. Help me to share
all that I have with others. Amen.*

Mending a Broken Heart

*Their insults have broken my heart, and I am
in despair. If only one person would show some
pity; if only one would turn and comfort me.*
PSALM 69:20 NLT

When your heart is broken, you feel sad and vulnerable. Being vulnerable does not mean you are weak, however. In God's hands, your vulnerability is an amazing strength. It is a witness to your deep connection to the Creator and a voice that soothes the wounds of others.

If your heart is broken by insults or rejection, go back to the Source of your strength. Go back to your Father and put your hand in His. Tell Him all that you feel; give Him all the pieces so that He can help you mend again.

When you do, you will be restored. A restored and renewed spirit can then take the challenges of the world head-on and heart-first. Thank God that He always mends a broken heart.

*Lord, thank You for being there for me, for protecting
my heart and mending my spirit. Help me
to heal and move on quickly. Amen.*

God Wants First Place

Dear children, keep away from anything that
might take God's place in your hearts.
1 JOHN 5:21 NLT

Everything in your life demands your attention. Many things need your focus and deserve to have priority. However, God knows you far better than anyone else can ever know you. He knows what you need, oftentimes before you know. He gives you grace, mercy, and peace, and He always has your back. He doesn't want to be number one for His sake. He wants to be number one for your sake! No one else can provide for you, love you, or direct your steps like He can.

Today, as you share your love with your family and friends, take time to honor the One who gives all things to you in the first place and who seeks after your good in every way. Give God the first place in your heart.

Lord, help me to love my family in all the ways You've
given me to love them, and then let me love You
and worship You like no other. Amen.

Every Time I Feel the Spirit

Be filled with the Spirit. Speak to each other with psalms,
hymns, and spiritual songs, singing and making
music in your hearts to the Lord.
EPHESIANS 5:18–19 NCV

Have you had any of those great moments lately where you just feel the Spirit of God in your heart and soul? You know, the sense that you are so overcome with the joy of knowing God's love is in you that you almost feel giddy and can do nothing else but rejoice and sing and pray.

If that hasn't happened to you lately, maybe it's time to figure out why not. The Spirit is available to you *all* the time, so having His Spirit move yours can be a fairly common occurrence. It just requires more focus and a slight change of your heart.

Don't wait for a feeling to come over you. Just start those prayers of thanksgiving, humming those great spiritual songs and singing your heart out to the Lord. When you do that, your heart will rejoice because your spirit is moving.

Lord, dance with me today as I lift my voice in prayer and
praise to You. Move within my being, so that my heart
and mind can shine Your light of love. Amen.

The First to Forgive

How great is God's love for all who worship him?
Greater than the distance between heaven and earth!
How far has the LORD taken our sins from us?
Farther than the distance from east to west!
PSALM 103:11–12 CEV

We're funny about forgiveness. If we need forgiveness, we want the instant kind that makes all the bad stuff go away quickly. Drop in a forgiveness tablet, watch it fizz, presto. . .no more problem. That's what we'd like when we're the ones needing forgiveness.

When we're the ones doing the forgiving, well, that's another matter. That's something that weighs on our hearts and causes us to make excuses. God wants you to recognize how often He forgives you and how far away from Himself He puts your offenses. He wants us to follow His example, and there's no way to do that unless you get your heart involved.

Be the first to forgive; it will do your heart good.

Lord, grant me the willingness to forgive, be forgiven,
and let go of past injuries. Help me move forward
today with a more loving heart. Amen.

Putting on the Armor

Be strong in the Lord and in his mighty power.
Put on the full armor of God, so that you can
take your stand against the devil's schemes.
EPHESIANS 6:10–11 NIV

When you go through your closet to find the stuff you've outgrown so you can give it away to a charity, be sure you don't throw out your armor. . . .

It's in there somewhere—your protective coating against the prowler who often wears sheep's clothing, just to catch you off guard. It's Spirit ready, and no matter what, it will keep you standing in God's strength and direction. In fact, it's indestructible armor and it was designed with you in mind.

So get rid of those old shirts from college that you're never going to really wear anyway, and let go of those old worn-out tennis shoes, but never give away your armor. It is one of God's ways of protecting your heart and your soul, and you will need it any minute. Stay strong in the Lord.

Lord, protect me as I go into the world today.
Keep me strong in Your mighty power. Amen.

Becoming a Wise Old Soul

My child, listen to what I say, and treasure my commands. Tune your ears to wisdom, and concentrate on understanding. Cry out for insight, and ask for understanding. Search for them as you would for silver; seek them like hidden treasures.

PROVERBS 2:1–4 NLT

As we strive to live a more heart-shaped life, it is important that we seek God's guidance about things that will make us wiser—not necessarily smarter, but wiser. After all, things of this world will not give us greater intelligence or common sense. God alone is at the heart of all wisdom and is your greatest Source to becoming a wiser person.

It's a new day and a new chance to pay attention to your choices. Look at the reasons behind what you do, and pray for wisdom in making your decisions. Let your head analyze your choices, and let your heart clarify your motivations. When you do, you'll discover some great treasures and become a wise old soul in all the things that truly matter to the heart.

Lord, grant me greater insight and understanding about the choices I make. Create in me a desire to be wise in all matters of the heart. Amen.

Living a Life of Perfect Love

God is love, and all who live in love live in God,
and God lives in them. And as we live in
God, our love grows more perfect.
1 JOHN 4:16–17 NLT

Today, remember that God's love lives within you and it will remain with you forever. You cannot put it out like a flaming candlewick or lose it by your own neglect. You can only seek to know more of it and strive to see it in each person you meet, each desire of your heart, and each fervent prayer. God's love prevails and you have every reason to trust it and to know that He will love you and live with you eternally.

May He continue to shape your heart to see beauty in others and shape your spirit to want even more of all that He desires for you. Live in God and in His love from now to forever.

Lord, thank You for living in my heart and soul.
Help me to seek even more of You in
everything I do today. Amen.

The Friendship Factor

There was an immediate bond between them,
for Jonathan loved David.
1 SAMUEL 18:1 NLT

C. S. Lewis said, "Friendship is born at that moment when one person says to another, 'What? You too? I thought I was the only one.' " It's important to have people in our lives who relate to the life lessons we've learned or who understand our goals and our heart's desires. Those are the people who sustain us when the hard times come along, holding us up in prayer and keeping us firmly planted in their hearts. These are the people who make a difference in our everyday existence.

Today is a good day to honor your friendships. Thank God for each of the people in your life who have shaped your heart by their kindness and love. No doubt, they thank God for you as well.

Lord, I thank You for my dear friends and even
the acquaintances who support my spirit,
give me a hand, and strengthen my dreams.
Please bless each of their lives today. Amen.

When the Light Goes Out

"This is what the Lord All-Powerful says: 'Do what is right and true. Be kind and merciful to each other.'"
ZECHARIAH 7:9 NCV

When we're left in the dark, we look to God to sustain us and we look to our friends to help us find the light again. The important thing to remember is that wherever you are, you may run across someone in that uncertain place, just sitting in the dark, waiting for you to turn the light on again. You know you lead a heart-shaped life when you are aware of the needs of others and have a great desire to help those who are lost.

Ask God to go with you and show you where you can shed the light of kindness on another human being. After all, God knew you'd come along just when you did. He's counting on you to reach out to share your heart and to reach up to shine His light.

Lord, when my light goes out, I am grateful for others who help me find my way again. Fill my heart with a desire to do any kindness I can do today. Amen.

A Garden of Goodness

Their life will be like a watered garden,
and all their sorrows will be gone.
JEREMIAH 31:12 NLT

Jeremiah talks about life in a watered garden. Water is the life force, the nourisher of the soil, and the life giver of the garden. A mix of water and sunshine will ensure that the garden will produce great bounty and, in one sense, feed its caretakers.

Your heart is like a garden as well, for from it comes the wellspring of life, wisdom, and goodness. It is the place where simple joys have meaning; the place that welcomes what life brings, balancing the rains and the sunshine.

When your heart is a well-watered garden, it is nourishing and refreshing to your spirit. If it isn't, then see if there are things that need to be raked and cleaned up, so you can start growing again. God will bless all your efforts.

Lord, help me to grow in You and nurture those in my
care according to Your design for our lives. Amen.

God at Work. . .in You!

For God is working in you, giving you the desire
and the power to do what pleases him.
PHILIPPIANS 2:13 NLT

You are important to God and your work for Him makes a difference. You're His hands, feet, voice, and heart, and He counts on you to get His job done. God walks beside you, listens to you, and stays close to you because, together, you're a force to be reckoned with.

One reason God "needs" you is because He enjoys being around you and seeing you delight in His continual blessings. He especially enjoys seeing you come to life when you're doing good deeds, helping others, and offering Him thanks for all you have. God's need of you is about designing a relationship of love with Him so that you can then live a life of joy in all you do for others.

It's a new day. Give God a chance to work wonders in your heart!

Lord, thank You for all the good things You do in my life,
and help me to never doubt that You and I together
can make a difference in the world. Amen.

Slightly Used Pots

And yet, O Lord, you are our Father. We are the clay,
and you are the potter. We all are formed by your hand.
ISAIAH 64:8 NLT

What do you see when you look in the mirror? Once you get past the idea that you're getting older and you're working harder than ever to stay in shape, then you need to look further. You need to wait there long enough to see the "you" that God sees. You need to see the one the Lord loves and nurtures. You are being molded, shaped, and smoothed a bit more every day by His almighty, loving hands. You are becoming all that He meant for you to become. You are beautiful clay in the hands of a master Potter.

As you look again then, you should see one of the most beautiful creations on earth. You should see a unique person, with a heart shaped and molded to do wonderful things for your Father in heaven. The Potter is proud of you.

Lord, renew my heart in You, and shape me so I can see
myself with Your eyes and be encouraged to try
again to be all You've made me to be. Amen.

Discovering the Difference

Humble yourselves before the Lord,
and he will lift you up in honor.
JAMES 4:10 NLT

Acceptance of things we cannot change takes courage. Often, we spend countless hours trying to discover how to solve a problem or how to change a situation, only to finally arrive at the place that prayerfully understands we have to be at peace with some things as they are.

Working for change also takes courage because obstacles must be overcome and new paths must be discovered. It takes courage to stand up for a cause or to try to improve an otherwise difficult situation. It takes courage to live heart-first.

Knowing the difference takes wisdom, and wisdom means that you put your circumstances before the Lord and admit your dependence on Him. The God of peace, courage, and wisdom will change your heart and help you discover the difference He alone can make.

Lord, I seek Your peace and guidance in all situations
where I struggle to make a difference. Shape my
heart to desire Your will in all things. Amen.

The Winds of Change

"May the LORD bless you and protect you. May the LORD smile on you and be gracious to you. May the LORD show you his favor and give you his peace."

NUMBERS 6:24–26 NLT

The winds of change are stirring around you for a reason. They are blowing opportunities right into your path and hoping you'll gather them up and do something about them. Change cannot happen on its own. It needs a constant force behind it, and if you find that a passion is brewing within your heart to get something done, then God may well be appointing you to the task.

Being the change that helps shape new direction and new perspective isn't easy, but when you work for God, He will open doors to help those changes take place. God will favor you with His peace and bless you with the necessary change of heart to embrace His work for the good of others.

Lord, make it clear to my heart when I need to be an agent for change, and grant me Your peace. Amen.

Weeds of Worry

*Humble yourselves, therefore, under God's mighty hand,
that he may lift you up in due time. Cast all your
anxiety on him because he cares for you.*
1 PETER 5:6–7 NIV

Worries come at us from every direction, and if we uproot one, another comes from nowhere and plants itself firmly in its place. Before we know it, we feel suffocated by life and wonder why we aren't feeling the sunshine on our faces. We need God's help to reshape our thinking and give us hearts of joy.

You may not be able to keep worry from sprouting or even from coming into full bloom, but you can decide what you'll do when it comes along. You can hand it over to the Master Gardener and let Him deal with it. Your job then is simply to keep growing right where you are and let Him handle the rest. Before long, you may not even notice a stray worry that comes in because the Gardener will take care of it before you even know it's there.

*Lord, I know that worry tends to steal my peace any
chance it gets. Help me to weed it out of my life and
hand it over to You as quickly as possible. Amen.*

Round Pegs and Square Holes

This is the day that the LORD has made;
let us rejoice and be glad in it.
PSALM 118:24 ESV

As God continues to give you a heart-shaped life, He inspires you to think in new ways. You see things from a perspective that you never understood before. You think with your head, but you move past that and check in with your heart. You simply live differently. You may feel like a round peg in a square hole, but that's okay.

You're on a path of discovery. Reach up and connect to the Source of your light and love and let Him show you where you'll fit the best. All the good things are getting better. Your heart will guide you to a place of true joy. Celebrate all that life brings you today and give God the glory!

Lord, I'm growing and changing, and sometimes I'm afraid
of what that means. Help me to move in the direction
that will bring us both great joy! Amen.

Bend, Don't Break!

I love the LORD because he hears my voice and my prayer for mercy. Because he bends down to listen, I will pray as long as I have breath!
PSALM 116:1–2 NLT

Physical exercise is about stretching and bending. Spiritual exercise is about stepping out and stepping up to follow Jesus. It's about surrendering your heart to the One who can really make a difference in your life.

Some of us are not very flexible. We cannot bend very far without serious consequences. We're comfortable, and getting nudged out of our comfort zone doesn't make us happy.

God wants you to reach a little further than your grasp today. Exercise some greater opportunities to serve His people. Lift someone from their suffering or hug someone with the spirit of warmth and caring if you want to do some bending exercises. It's so much easier to bend than it is to break.

The Lord listens to your heart, softens it, and makes it more flexible to handle the needs of others. If you bend with your heart, it won't get broken.

Lord, I am still learning to give over the things I think and feel so that I can create more opportunities to love others as You would have me do. Help my heart become more flexible. Amen.

The Clouds Are Gathering

Examine yourselves to see if your faith is genuine.
Test yourselves. Surely you know that Jesus Christ
is among you; if not, you have failed
the test of genuine faith.

2 Corinthians 13:5 NLT

God has a plan for you and He won't let go of it. It may seem that He's keeping a distance or He's giving you time to work things out for yourself. Keep praying and keep checking to see if He's nearby and you'll discover that He's been there all along, guiding you and shaping your direction.

If you've been walking through stormy times, just keep walking because God is already ahead of you waiting to help you, waiting to heal you. He is there standing in the light and will shine it on you to direct your path.

If your faith is in need of a heart transplant, ask God to help you. Ask Him to give you a heart like His, steadfast and genuine. He will sustain you no matter what life brings your way.

Lord, please keep walking with me on this journey of
life. I'm not always sure I can see which way to go,
so I'm counting on You to lead me and
shine a light on my path. Amen.

Why We Have Hope

*We also glory in our sufferings, because we
know that suffering produces perseverance;
perseverance, character; and character, hope.*
ROMANS 5:3–4 NIV

God's love is the reason you have hope. When you face a trial and find your comfort in God's arms and your direction in His Word, then your hope rises again. You know that you are never alone and that nothing can happen to you that He does not know.

When you keep going, keep trusting, keep believing in what He has planned, then your character is ever stronger and your hope is alive. You do not have the hope of those who wish on stars in the heavens. You have the hope of those who believe in the Son of God and the gifts that only the heavenly Father bestows. Rejoice in your sufferings and even more in your hope, and let your heart be glad. Receive His love today.

*Lord, thank You for always being with me,
my everlasting Hope and loving Heart. Amen.*

Counting Your Blessings

Let us draw near to God with a sincere heart and
with the full assurance that faith brings.

HEBREWS 10:22 NIV

Thank God for watching over you and for giving you the strength, energy, and presence of mind to begin a new day. Seek His will and His presence for each decision you have to make and each step you take.

This is your day to count it all joy when you see His face in others and when you reflect His grace to those around you. He sees you and knows you. He guides you and blesses you with a complete assurance that He has your back and that your prayers are heard.

When you live a heart-shaped life, it is always a good day to draw near to God in the full assurance of faith. He will sustain you all through the day and keep your heart in alignment with His own.

Lord, help me to always want to be close to You,
learning from You and growing in faith because
of You. Bless my heart and my efforts to
bless others in return. Amen.

Try to Be Helpful

---

*Don't get tired of helping others. You will be
rewarded when the time is right, if you don't give
up. We should help people whenever we can,
especially if they are followers of the Lord.*
GALATIANS 6:9–10 CEV

The writer of Galatians reminds us that we may be tired, but we shouldn't give up. We have to remember the needs of others. We're God's heart and His hands in the world.

When you offer a word of solace, give a gift of love, or lend a hand, people's lives are blessed and so is yours. Your kindness makes a difference, and your generous spirit shows you are a child of God.

Kindness opens doors, embraces weaker souls, and encourages those who may be downhearted. Think of how often someone else's kindness made a difference to you. Be helpful! Smile! Try to never grow weary of doing good things for others.

---

*Lord, bless those I meet today, and remind me to offer
a little kindness wherever I can. Help me to share
Your light and Your generous Spirit. Amen.*

It Only Takes a Spark

"For God loves a person who gives cheerfully."
2 CORINTHIANS 9:7 NLT

We sometimes neglect doing the little things because we don't recognize how important they are. Your small gift, whether it's a smile, a sandwich, or the match that lights a fire, is the spark that changes lives. Your spark can light up the world. A single coal trying to burn on its own will ultimately burn out, but when it is placed together with other coals, fires of possibility warm everyone around.

God has given you a heart to make a difference and the opportunities, in big ways and small ways, to share His love with others. Be the match that lights someone else's way. Carry the torch of God's love for others and pass it along wherever you are.

Lord, help me to share Your love with others today and make a difference in any way that I can. Bless my little efforts and multiply the joys they bring. Amen.

Gifts of the Heart

Do to others as you would like them to do to you.
LUKE 6:31 NLT

When you stand for a cause, give to a friend, or add expertise that gets a job done, then it brings an opportunity for celebration. Giving makes you feel good. God blessed you with very specific gifts so that you could share them. He puts you in the exact right circumstances so your heart is touched by what you can contribute to bring joy to the situation.

You offer heartfelt prayers on behalf of others, words of encouragement, and do good deeds in the Lord's service. You show that God has indeed shaped your heart to love those around you. Thank God for giving you His love and a heart that is so willing to be a gift to others.

Lord, You have given so much to me. Thank You for
any opportunity I may have to give back
to others in Your name. Amen.

The "Getting" Frenzy

"You should remember the words of the Lord Jesus:
'It is more blessed to give than to receive.'"

ACTS 20:35 NLT

♥

Winston Churchill said, "We make a living by what we get. We make a life by what we give." Most of us think more about the getting than the giving, and we may not even realize we have that focus. Remember that even if you don't have all the latest technological gadgets, if you sleep in a warm bed at night, eat dinner on a regular basis, and have clean water to drink, you're living in a state of wealth. You have more toys than a good share of the world enjoys.

Be grateful, and thank God with your whole heart for His mercy and provision. Then let God shape your heart and spur you on to greater giving on behalf of those in need. Let your giving become a lasting blessing wherever you are.

Lord, I praise You for the provisions You have
made in my life. Help me to share all that I have
according to the direction of Your Spirit. Amen.

A Heart for All Seasons

There is a time for everything, and a season
for every activity under the heavens.
ECCLESIASTES 3:1 NIV

Friendship requires an interesting set of heart skills to make it work well. You have to know when to jump in with your advice and your good intentions and when to back off and let your friend figure out things alone. You have to know when to share a laugh, a hug, a moment, or when to listen with your heart. Friends carry burdens together, and sometimes friends stand apart or step back.

The key is that friendship is all about love and about giving. You give love, energy, time, thoughtfulness, and strength. You give separation, silence, and prayer. You give from the heart because that's what God made you to do.

As you think about your close friends today, honor them before God, and give Him praise for the many joys you share.

Lord, my friend is so important to me and I'm not always
sure how to best take care of her needs. Help me to
be as giving and tender as possible today. Amen.

The Dimmer Switch

A friend is always loyal, and a brother
is born to help in time of need.
PROVERBS 17:17 NLT

In any friendship, the roles are constantly being reversed. The heart of friendship is about offering strength in time of need, or simply being there to hold a hand. Friendship turns on the light, turns up the light, or turns out the light, depending on the situation. Friendship, then, is like a dimmer switch and when it's plugged into the Source of Light Himself, it can make an amazing difference. Friends with great hearts help each other see everything more clearly. When they stick together, God blesses them both with even more love and admiration.

Celebrate your friends. Enjoy the delightful fact that God loves you so much, He provided very special people to show you His love each day.

Lord, thank You for blessing me with friends who
strengthen me, laugh with me, and help shape
my life in worthwhile ways. Bless each of the
friends You've given me today. Amen.

It's All Possible!

"All things are possible for one who believes."
MARK 9:23 ESV

Hope and love will get you on the right path, and with practice and perseverance you'll get where you were designed to go. All things are possible, but sometimes God makes you the catalyst. You have to find the way around the obstacles, have faith through setbacks, and continue on even when you've failed. You have to believe your objective is possible to achieve.

When you have put the desires of your heart before God and have waited with patience and trusted that things would come together, but nothing happens, you may be missing one ingredient. You may need to believe God will act on your behalf for one reason and one reason only. . .because He utterly adores you. Only with Him are all things possible.

Lord, it is hard to pursue my dreams when they don't come together for a long time. Please help me to patiently hope and believe that they are yet to be, according to Your will and purpose. Amen.

Intentional Living

For everything, absolutely everything, above and below,
visible and invisible...everything got started
in him and finds its purpose in him.
COLOSSIANS 1:16 MSG

You have a purpose, and there's no one who can accomplish the work you are meant to do but you. You're on a mission, and everyone else you know is on a mission as well.

God searches the hearts of His children so He can create clear paths to helping each one fulfill His purposes. Your goals and your heart's desires are all ways God achieves success in meeting the needs of people everywhere. He works through you and shapes your heart to do that work with love and mercy. He knows every detail and what it will take, and so He wants you to draw near to Him for strength and for wisdom. His intention is for you to succeed in every good way. Work with Him and fulfill your purpose in Him.

Lord, help me to fulfill the purpose You planned for me
and to do my life work with joy. Amen.

Prayers of the Heart

In the same way, the Spirit helps us in our weakness.
We do not know what we ought to pray for, but the
Spirit himself intercedes for us through wordless groans.
And he who searches our hearts knows the mind of
the Spirit, because the Spirit intercedes for God's
people in accordance with the will of God.
ROMANS 8:26–27 NIV

Sometimes we're not certain how to approach God because the concerns of our hearts are heavy and we don't know what words will get God's attention. When your heart is open to God and ready to seek His help, the words are not important. It's the condition of your heart and the willingness to be open and honest with God that truly makes the difference.

If you are a prayer person, God can easily hear your heart because He knows already what you are trying to say. He knows your needs even more than you may know them yourself. If you aren't certain that you know what to say when you come before God, you can be sure that He sees you coming and is ready to listen and respond.

Lord, I'm so grateful that You understand the complexities
of my life and the concerns of my heart. Please receive
my prayers with Your gracious love. Amen.

Abundant Living

Always be full of joy in the Lord. I say it again—rejoice!
Let everyone see that you are considerate in all you do.
PHILIPPIANS 4:4–5 NLT

Many of us have minds that are full of clutter, and the best thing we can do is give them a clean sweep.

When your thoughts are happy, positive, and full of grace, you're a different person. You're more productive, you're more fun to be around, and you give without even thinking, to provide for the needs of others. You live a heart-shaped life because all is well with your soul.

If you could learn to think better thoughts, you might learn to create better actions. God started the universe as a thought, then He spoke it into existence. His thoughts had enormous power. Your thoughts and your actions are powerful in a lot of ways too. Let joy fill your thoughts and offer you the best responses to life that the grace of God makes possible.

Lord, I don't stop to thank You enough for the
great joys in my life. I will think more about those
things today and praise Your name. Amen.

Find It in Your Heart

*No, the word is very near you; it is in your mouth
and in your heart so you may obey it.*
DEUTERONOMY 30:14 NIV

When you're ready to pray, check in with your heart. Look to see if it is indeed focused on the Lord Himself. Discover whether it is prepared to talk to the Creator of the whole universe. Set yourself apart with a time and a place where your heart can speak freely and your love can flow. Give yourself a place that is quiet and holy, a place for you and the Lord to truly communicate.

It's not difficult to understand the Word of God because He has already placed its very essence in your heart and He knows you by name. Call Him when you have prepared your heart to listen to His voice. It's the most important way to discover how to live a heart-shaped life.

*Lord, help me to prepare my heart to listen to You and to
seek Your guidance in all that I do this day. Amen.*

It's Us vs. Them

Yet we hear that some of you are living idle lives,
refusing to work and meddling in other people's business.
We command such people and urge them in the
name of the Lord Jesus Christ to settle down
and work to earn their own living.
2 THESSALONIANS 3:11–12 NLT

When we set ourselves up as the judge and jury for our neighbors, coworkers, or anyone else, we come to some pretty wrong conclusions. We may imagine that we're on one side of a fence and they are on the other; it's us versus them!

When you think like that, it may be time to check in with God and seek His help in shaping your heart then and there. You may be the one who needs to get things right so that life can be much better. You may be in need of a heart transplant.

When your heart is right with God, He guides you into His will and purpose, and you can be sure He focuses on what *you* need to change, not what *they* need to change. Ask Him to direct your thoughts and your heart.

Lord, I often expect others to take care of life the
same way I would. Help me to see them and love
them as You do and stop trying to judge the
differences between us. Amen.

Bless the Loaves and Fish!

*Jesus took the five loaves and two fish,
looked up toward heaven, and blessed them.*
MATTHEW 14:19 NLT

The example of Jesus was to receive God's blessing or offer a prayer of thanks before every meal. His example showed us that we should thank God for providing the food we eat and the basic necessities of life. When Jesus blessed the bread, there seemed to always be more of it to share. Even five loaves and two fish could feed multitudes when he needed it to do so.

Before you consume one more bite of Mom's chicken Kiev or Dad's grilled salmon, turn your heart and mind to the Giver of all life and all nourishment and thank Him. After you do, you can be sure that everything you taste will have an especially inviting flavor, and the blessings will flow.

*Lord, bless the food that I share with those around
me today. Thank You for taking such good
care of my basic needs. Amen.*

Head and Shoulders above the Rest

*Rather, you must grow in the grace and knowledge
of our Lord and Savior Jesus Christ.*

2 PETER 3:18 NLT

You may have excellent head knowledge of the Bible. You may know every scripture and just when to say it in the right context, but you may not have a good grasp of God's Word. Knowing scripture changes the way your heart perceives others, the way you act, and the way you speak. God speaks to your heart and searches the motives of your heart. He cares more about the motivations behind what you do than about the actions you decide to take.

It's a good day to seek God's heart and stand tall with Him. You're already head and shoulders above the rest because you have been searching for Him with your mind. As you engage Him more fully with your heart, you will see more clearly and grow in the special favor of the Lord.

*Lord, help me to take my head knowledge and
move it into heart knowledge. Amen.*

No Longer a Child

When I was a child, I talked like a child, I thought like
a child, I reasoned like a child. When I became a
man, I put the ways of childhood behind me.
1 CORINTHIANS 13:11 NIV

It's okay to grow up. In fact, it's a lifetime project. You may even be too adult in some ways, and still a kid in others. It's a process! Growing, changing, and learning are part of God's design to help us become more Christlike.

Augustine of Hippo put it this way: "If you are pleased with what you are, you have stopped already. If you say, 'It is enough,' you are lost. Keep on walking, moving forward, trying for the goal. Don't try to stop on the way, or to go back, or to deviate from it."

Because you're no longer a child, you have only one choice, and that is to keep walking and moving forward. Let your heart and mind lead you to Jesus and cause you to believe all that He makes possible.

Dear Lord, help me walk forward to the place You
would have me go with a heart that is mature in
You and a faith that remains childlike. Amen.

Broken Pottery

And yet, O Lord, you are our Father. We are the clay,
and you are the potter. We all are formed by your hand.
ISAIAH 64:8 NLT

Sometimes you may feel like a lump of clay, with no real form or special beauty. You don't know what your direction is and you feel like you're without purpose or motivation. You want God to shape you up.

When you surrender to being God's design, you may still have setbacks or feel utterly broken. Other times, you may also have a sense that you are functioning at a high level and are strengthened by the Potter's hand. Whether you feel broken or beautiful, remember that you are always lovingly being formed by the Master who sees your heart and knows exactly the beautiful vessel you need to be for His purpose.

Lord, I pray that You would shape my mind, body,
and spirit with Your loving hand today. Amen.

The Reality of Hope

Faith shows the reality of what we hope for;
it is the evidence of things we cannot see.
HEBREWS 11:1 NLT

Hope, coupled with the faith we have in Jesus Christ, changes our hearts and gives us strength. It helps us to see that we can trust and believe God in all we do. We can look to God to take care of the details of our lives, and so hope remains. The Hope of the Ages is with us every day, watching over us, and challenging us to be faithful and strong.

Today, think about the things you hoped for yesterday, and give God thanks and praise for honoring those hopes or pray again for the desires of your heart. Your hope will then carry the blessing and assurance of God's hand at work in you.

Father, there are many times when I fear I will lose
hope. Then You come into my life in a powerful way
and remind me that You are always with me.
Thank You for Your steadfast love. Amen.

Creating the Right Heart

*You must love the LORD your God with all your heart,
all your soul, all your mind, and all your strength.*
MARK 12:30 NLT

We're in the business then of setting our hearts right. Jesus stated it another way when he said that we should seek God with all of our heart, mind, and soul. Perhaps in seeking God, we may cultivate our personal life in a way that pleases God and sets our hearts right.

Today is a great day to do some housecleaning. Give yourself a chance to sweep out cobwebs of doubt and worry. Ask God to help you create a more loving heart so that you can improve the future by creating a present that serves God and others. Set your heart on God the Father and He will continue to shape it with love.

*Lord, create a clean heart in me today, and renew
a right spirit within me so that I can love
You and serve You more fully. Amen.*

Follow Your Heart

*"For the LORD sees every heart and knows every plan
and thought. If you seek him, you will find him."*
1 CHRONICLES 28:9 NLT

If you seek God, you will find Him. He will turn toward you and meet you halfway. He will never leave you in an uncertain path, for as soon as you call out to Him, He's there. If there's a longing in your heart today to do something you've never done, go someplace you've never been, or simply to change a habit or your life direction, then it's a good day to follow your heart.

Ask God to go before you, to guide your steps, and to bring you to the place that only He can to give you your heartfelt desires. Offer Him thanks and praise for all the ways He will meet you to make your dreams come true. Go ahead and follow your heart!

*Lord, it isn't always easy to figure out the next steps
or the wisest course of action. Help me to follow my
heart to You to create each step according
to Your wisdom for me. Amen.*

The Heart of Honesty

"As for you, if you walk before me faithfully with integrity
of heart and uprightness. . .and do all I command and
observe my decrees and laws, I will establish
your royal throne over Israel forever."

1 KINGS 9:4–5 NIV

Somewhere along the way, a lot of people have forgotten the values they learned in childhood. They've forgotten that it's still important to tell the truth and to be honest with others.

Sure, you can get away with those little untruths where you pretend to like your boss's funky tie or your mom's new haircut. You can even refrain from speaking out when you're struggling with honest emotions. Your heart knows when it is being honest and when it is unwilling to speak the truth.

If honesty is to remain a virtue, then we've got to give it a chance and deliver it ourselves. You'll be glad when you work harder to authentically share your heart. . . honest!

Lord, let honesty come from my heart and my lips in
all my actions and interactions with others. . .
and especially with You. Amen.

The Heart of Forgiveness

Be kind to each other, tenderhearted, forgiving one another, just as God through Christ has forgiven you.
EPHESIANS 4:32 NLT

Forgiveness is a matter of the heart that is unlike any other. It brings change and acceptance to both the giver and the receiver.

Rude and crude and mean and nasty have all been out there for some time and are having a field day at our expense. Isn't it time to combat them with big doses of kindness, generous amounts of forgiveness, and love whenever you have the chance? As one writer put it, "To understand is not only to pardon, but in the end to love."

If you want to be part of the change you'd like to see in the world, then let the grace of God rule in your heart in such a way that you can share His forgiveness for all human beings with great joy. Forgiving yourself and others lightens your steps like nothing else can do.

Lord, I know You have forgiven me over and over again. Help me to be more tenderhearted toward others and seek to follow Your forgiving example. Amen.

Glory to God

Our faces, then, are not covered. We all show the Lord's glory, and we are being changed to be like him. This change in us brings ever greater glory, which comes from the Lord, who is the Spirit.

2 CORINTHIANS 3:18 NCV

You look a lot like your Father! Now that's the most beautiful thing that can ever be said about you when you acknowledge and know your Father in heaven. You let your light radiate in ways that you could never have believed possible. You want to do this because God has turned His face to shine upon you and you have opened your heart to see Him.

Remember always that you are walking in greater joy each day as you walk in the Spirit, for God covers you with His glory and gives you His eyes to see the world. May God light your way wherever you go today.

Lord, thank You for shining the light of Your love on me. Help me to share in Your glory and offer that same radiance and joy to those around me. Amen.

See Your Neighbor

"Love your neighbor as yourself."
MATTHEW 19:19 NIV

See if you can actually get to know someone new today. Be intentional about meeting people you have barely known and show them what God has done in your life. Ask them to share the ways God has shown up in their lives. Encourage each other's hearts and minds.

Find out the name of your mail carrier, your dry cleaner, or the paperboy. The older man who walks by your house every day has a name. The grocer and the guy who picks up the trash do too. Practice making yourself and your neighbors more visible.

If you sincerely get to know those around you, your heart will grow and no one will be invisible. Today, share your love and your joy in Jesus.

Lord, I confess I don't know my neighbors very well, but I know how loneliness feels, and I ask You to help me be better at getting to know the people in my neighborhood. Amen.

Good-Hearted You

Do not withhold good from those who deserve it when it's in your power to help them. If you can help your neighbor now, don't say, "Come back tomorrow, and then I'll help you."
PROVERBS 3:27-28 NLT

Perhaps the most powerful person you know is the neighbor who welcomes family, friends, and even strangers to her table. Perhaps it's the woman who loves with her whole heart, or the man who generously gives his time, money, or labor without ever asking for anything in return.

Real power, then, may be the strength that comes from a good heart, the impact of a kind word or bit of advice, or the hand that reaches out when tragedy strikes. Real power is what you have inside your heart and mind because Jesus lives within you. Real power is made entirely of love. Rekindle your own power today. The more love you give away, the more you have. Funny, but you could have the strength of ten people just by showing love to others.

Lord, help me understand what real power is within me, and help me go after that power in the spirit of love. Amen.

Quiet Desperation

Every good and perfect gift comes down from the
Father who created all the lights in the heavens.

JAMES 1:17 CEV

What makes the difference between getting a life of quiet desperation and a life of abundance?

Desperation focuses on all that we lack, and worry fixes our minds on ourselves and not on the Lord. When we strive to live a heart-shaped life, then we have to trust and believe in possibility. With your heart open to abundance, you can see the good and perfect gifts coming to you from your Father in heaven.

Since you're the child of a King, abundance is all around you, and God wants to lavish you with love and all good things. He has a lot of gifts to give you, and if you don't feel that you're receiving them, it may be that you need to sit a little closer to His throne.

Lord, help me to believe that You have an intention
for good things for my life. Create a life of abundance
all around me, and strengthen my heart to accept
Your gifts of love and kindness. Amen.

Chasing the Wind

*It's better to enjoy what we have than to always
want something else, because that makes
no more sense than chasing the wind.*

ECCLESIASTES 6:9 CEV

It's good to seek new direction and learn about possibilities and ideas. It's good to keep growing and stimulating your imagination. Sometimes though, you get caught with your little net trying to chase dreams that you haven't fully prepared or planned. Sometimes you find yourself just chasing the wind.

Today is a good day to stop and check with God about your dreams and plans. See the beauty that exists right where you are now, and know that He is with you, shaping your heart to move you into a bright future. Start with a conversation with God and He'll help you know when to go after your dreams. Only with Him are you assured that you won't simply be chasing the wind.

*Lord, remind me to be thankful for all that I have at this
very moment, and to seek You with my whole heart to
discover all that is still mine to explore. Amen.*

A Heart to Remember

"The eye is the lamp of the body. If your eyes are healthy, your whole body will be full of light."
MATTHEW 6:22 NIV

Sometimes it's good to start the day by simply remembering a few worthwhile things. Maybe these can get you started:

- ♥ Your kindness brings power.
- ♥ Your wisdom brings peace.
- ♥ Your heart brings love.
- ♥ Your work brings joy.
- ♥ Your perseverance brings patience.
- ♥ Your helping hand brings gentleness.
- ♥ Your prayer life brings self-control.
- ♥ Your daily Bible reading brings goodness.
- ♥ Your desire to please God brings faithfulness.

Your life is in God's hands. Let your head, your heart, and your eyes be full of light.

Lord, thank You for bringing real joy into my life through the gifts of Your ever-present Spirit. Shape my heart to always see Your love and light. Amen.

Better Times

Many people say, "Who will show us better times?"
Let your face smile on us, LORD. You have given
me greater joy than those who have abundant
harvests of grain and new wine.
PSALM 4:6–7 NLT

You are incredibly blessed because every time you pray, every time you seek to draw closer to God, you have the smile of His face shining down on you. His radiating smile and steadfast love zero in on you. His love gives you greater joy than all the jewels at Tiffany's or all the grapes in the Sonoma Valley. You've got the best and the brightest, and nothing begins to compare with it.

If you're living in the shadows today, then it's time to come back out into the light and give God the glory. You're set to sparkle! You're set to have better times, and all you have to do is pray. Now that should make your heart skip a beat!

Lord, there is nothing more wonderful than sharing
in Your light. Thanks for giving me Your grace
and mercy and for helping me maintain
some luster in Your presence. Amen.

Light Show

Make your light shine, so that others will see the good that you do and will praise your Father in heaven.
MATTHEW 5:16 CEV

As a child of God, you have light to share, and others are in need of it. You may indeed be the candle, the floodlight, the flashlight—something that shines directly on those around you. You may also simply hold up the mirror of grace and with genuine kindness share your faithful light with others.

You don't have to be an evangelist, a church leader, or a lighthouse to be a beacon to those in need. You just have to have a willing heart to let your light shine so that others can discover the Source of your joy and inspiration.

Today, be a candle of inspiration, a beam of joy, a twinkle of blessing to someone around you. It can make a big difference to their heart and to yours.

Lord, help me shine Your light in positive, warm, and loving ways to those I encounter today. Amen.

Neighbors and Other Strangers

"Love your neighbor as yourself."
MARK 12:31 NIV

A word like *love* causes an emotional response between people and is the reason our hearts connect to each other. The same word can also cause a response toward something we just enjoy. . .like chocolate or cream puffs.

If you don't know your neighbors, or the neighbors next to them, or the ones across town, how are you supposed to love them? More than that, how do you love your neighbor as yourself?

As you consider this scripture, think about ways you can simply get to know your neighbors better. Maybe in getting to know and love your neighbors, you'll learn a little more about loving yourself as well.

Lord, it's not easy to make the effort to love people I don't know. Help me to be a better neighbor by seeing each person with a heart of love. Amen.

When You Reflect the Son

*You are like light for the whole world. . . . Make your
light shine, so that others will see the good that
you do and will praise your Father in heaven.*
MATTHEW 5:14, 16 CEV

♥

Your light is always available, and often it shines best in
the darkness. You were designed to fill in the dark spaces
and bring them light because you reflect the Son. You're
like turning the switch on so everyone can see more
clearly. You send your waves of love and grace out into
the world and hope that the darkness will embrace your
message. You are what it means to live a heart-shaped
life.

As a child of God, you carry the light to every corner
of the world that you encounter. You reflect Him like the
moon and shine for everyone to see, or you shine His
light like the sunshine and bring His warmth to those in
great need of it.

You can't help but shine! It's the reason God shaped
your heart with such love!

*Lord, it is such an honor to share Your grace and Your light
with others. I'm awed that You have blessed me
with the chance to be a twinkling star. Amen.*

The Spirit of Truth

When the Spirit of truth comes, he will guide you into all truth. He will not speak on his own but will tell you what he has heard. He will tell you about the future.

JOHN 16:13 NLT

To live for today requires us to line our hearts up with the guidance we receive from the Holy Spirit. The Spirit of Truth can share with us all that the Father has in mind. He can give us insight into the future and even into the present. Isn't that pretty incredible? We are worrying about the future, when we have a Guide right here and now.

If you're limping along, wondering if life is ever going to get you where you want to go, then stop what you're doing. Let go of every negative thought you have and surrender to the guidance of the Spirit of Truth. It won't be long and you'll have some very clear answers and a much happier heart.

Lord, it is awesome that You provide so well for my daily needs. You know everything about me, and so I come to You to claim more joy. Help me seek the Spirit of Truth today. Amen.

Putting Up with Each Other!

God loves you and has chosen you as his own special
people. So be gentle, kind, humble, meek, and patient.
Put up with each other, and forgive anyone who does
you wrong, just as Christ has forgiven you.
COLOSSIANS 3:12–13 CEV

This verse in Colossians helps us see that gentleness and humility are hallmarks that could let us give one another room to be who we are. Isn't that really what we all want? Don't we want to know that those around us accept us and love us just the way we are? Sure, we test their patience and we beg their forgiveness; it's all part of recognizing that God loves us and is working on us to make us better. He expects us to be patient with one another and love one another that way too.

As you practice kindness, gentleness, and humility, someone is sure to test you to see if you really mean it. You've been forgiven so that you can be a forgiving spirit in the world. Be gentle, there are a lot of battles going on out there. Everyone around you needs an encounter with someone who lives a more heart-shaped life.

Lord, help me to remember that other people put up with
me just as often as I put up with them. Whatever I do
today, help me to be full of Your kindness and love. Amen.

Love Talk

If I could speak all the languages of earth and of angels, but didn't love others, I would only be a noisy gong or a clanging cymbal.
1 CORINTHIANS 13:1 NLT

We need to do everything with a heart toward others. We need to do everything in love. We can have a PhD in science, math, or linguistics, but the language we speak and the work we do has no meaning apart from what our hearts are also doing. If your heart isn't connected to your work, you may as well be a noisy locomotive going uphill all the way.

The concept is simple enough, but the execution of it is not that easy. We take great pride in our successes, and that's okay as long as our goals are aligned with God's purpose and our hearts are reaching out to others.

Listen carefully to yourself today and try to discover your own love language. Are you a clanging cymbal or a symphony of love?

Lord, let me remember always that my real work involves loving those You've put into my life. Amen.

Worth Waiting For

The faithful love of the LORD never ends!
His mercies never cease. Great is his faithfulness;
his mercies begin afresh each morning.
LAMENTATIONS 3:22–23 NLT

Hebrews 10:36 (NLT) says, "Patient endurance is what you need now, so that you will continue to do God's will. Then you will receive all that he has promised."

Waiting on God's promise with patient endurance is the hard part. It often feels more like an endurance test than it does simply waiting. When your next decision really matters though, remember that the Lord's mercies are new every morning and that He is totally faithful to you. He is working to give you an open heart and mind so you recognize His hand in every decision you make. He will truly direct your steps if you give Him a chance.

He gives you unfailing, never-ending love, and He protects you when you seek His heart for the important matters of life.

Lord, help me today to wait patiently for You so I make good choices. Keep my heart aligned with Yours. Amen.

Lesson from Job

There once was a man named Job who lived in the land of Uz. He was blameless—a man of complete integrity.
JOB 1:1 NLT

We may not see all the land mines that are out there to try to hinder our walk with God, but He does, and it's important that we pay close attention.

Remaining faithful when you're bombarded with life's setbacks is a challenge. If you've had to face miseries over and over again, you begin to wonder if God really knows you're there and if He hears your prayers and pleas for help.

The answer is that He does know and He cares. He's with you to help you discover a new path. Embrace your life challenges with patient endurance, knowing full well that God protects your heart and has your back. Believe in God, and in yourself, and know that all good things will be restored to you soon. Ask God to give you a heart of complete integrity.

Lord, when life hands me bad news, I hardly know what to believe. Help me to keep trusting and believing in You. Shape my thoughts and my actions to live with great integrity. Amen.

In His Presence

You will show me the way of life, granting me the joy of your presence and the pleasures of living with you forever.
PSALM 16:11 NLT

Take a deep breath and think about what you can do when negative thinking looms. Try some of these ideas to spur you on toward greater patience and positive thinking in the presence of God:

P stands for peace, prayer, and positive spirit.
A stands for attitude adjustment.
T stands for thankfulness for all you have.
I stands for insight and imitating Christ.
E stands for expecting that all is well.
N stands for not giving in to negative thoughts.
C stands for caring about all those around you.
E stands for experiencing more of God's grace.

When you're vexed, seek God's presence and read this list again. God will make sure your needs are met. Maybe then you'll spell patience with joy, knowing you are always in His presence.

Lord, be with me today as I work through the things that keep me stirred up and unable to quietly feel Your presence. Amen.

God's Children

God blesses those people who make peace.
They will be called his children!
MATTHEW 5:9 CEV

How do we stand up and be counted as peacemakers and children of God? We become the warriors of prayer, vigilantly seeking God's help to bring peace in the world, in the communities where we live, and in the hearts of each person we meet. We surrender our need for things and embrace our need for one another. We become Samaritans of the universe, knowing that life itself depends on us. We are leaders who defend the good and create a place for future generations to exist.

Let peace rule in your heart today as you pray for peace everywhere on the globe. Let God shape your heart to have even greater compassion on others until the victory of peace is won. You are one of God's children and He welcomes your prayers for all humankind.

Lord, I know that many of Your children do not live in
a peaceful and safe environment. Remind me to
pray for them and for peace each day. Amen.

Bits of Wisdom

*Proverbs will teach you wisdom and self-control
and how to understand sayings with deep meanings.*
PROVERBS 1:2 CEV

Marketing gurus count on you to remember their product by the great slogans and catchphrases they use to persuade you to buy everything from car insurance to the latest technological gadget. Once you've purchased their product, they want you to talk about it, wear their slogan on a T-shirt, and get the news out to other potential buyers. This is the way we communicate things we're excited about in the world.

The book of Proverbs is similar to those slogans—full of bits of wisdom that you'll find useful and memorable. These are the slogans you'll recall when you need a good word; the ones that help keep you walking on the best path of life.

Open your heart today to exploring Proverbs, and commit one or two passages to memory. As Proverbs 1:7 (CEV) says, "Respect and obey the LORD! This is the beginning of knowledge. Only a fool rejects wisdom and good advice."

*Lord, grant me wisdom in understanding more of
the things that will help me live a life that honors
You. Teach me to be wise in all I do. Amen.*

The Hidden Treasure of Common Sense

*Keep in tune with wisdom and think what it means
to have common sense. Beg as loud as you can for
good common sense. Search for wisdom as you
would search for silver or hidden treasure.*
PROVERBS 2:2–4 CEV

Proverbs 2 grabs us and shakes us up a bit. It says, "Beg as loud as you can for good common sense." Even God knows we are apt to lose track of simple everyday commonsense things and that we'll have to call on Him to get them back. If you're a master at your computer but not so sure how to figure out your checkbook, or you're able to explain quantum theory to the masses, but you can't figure out what to wear with brown shoes, you're in a position to start begging. . .loudly!

Ask God to give you the kind of common sense that comes from the heart and acts in loving ways to those around you. Balance the savvy you have in doing a good job in the world with a degree of common sense wherever you are and you'll be truly blessed.

*Lord, I don't always do things in the most sensible way.
Help me to be wise in a very commonsense way, and help
me to do all things with the right heart. Amen.*

Advice about Advice

Without good advice everything goes wrong—
it takes careful planning for things to go right.
PROVERBS 15:22 CEV

When we're the ones seeking advice, we're open to a genuine response that may not fit with our hopes and plans. If we're just seeking confirmation of our own direction, then any advice will meet our needs because we won't take it to heart anyway.

When you give advice though, seek to do the loving thing. Seek to listen with ears attuned to the Holy Spirit, and speak with a voice that is pleasing to God.

Your advice can bring God's desires to someone's attention. If you've ever watched a friend or a family member make a bad choice and wished later that you had said something in spite of the risk, you understand the challenge of not giving a heartfelt word at the right time. After prayerful consideration, give your best advice with love.

Lord, help me to offer advice in a loving way when asked,
and to seek advice from those who will help guide
me according to Your will and purpose. Amen.

Today, Well Lived!

Don't brag about tomorrow!
Each day brings its own surprises.
PROVERBS 27:1 CEV

Yesterday cannot be reclaimed. Past joys, past friends, past relationships, are just that. . .passed on to the past! They are either to be enjoyed or let go so that you can truly live in today. Only God knows what tomorrow will bring, and so He doesn't need you to help figure things out.

Today is what God has given you. Today He has offered you the world, and He will rejoice if you live it well. Open your heart to this day with gusto! Be very conscious of seeing God's hand at work every place you go, and be His voice of love where you can. Live well today; it is a gift beyond measure.

Lord, thank You for loving me so much and giving
me the gift of today. Help me to use it
wisely and live it well. Amen.

Return to God Wholeheartedly

*"I will give them hearts that recognize me as the LORD.
They will be my people, and I will be their God,
for they will return to me wholeheartedly."*

JEREMIAH 24:7 NLT

You may have had moments when you forgot that God was there to help you. You went on alone, walking through life somewhat asleep, somewhat unaware of what you were missing. The light was within you, but it was dimmed by your own hand.

This is a great day to return to the Lord, the God of your heart. This is your day to shout for joy that He lives within you and that His light will shine forever, guiding your steps and ensuring that you are never alone.

Give God your heart one more time. Give it wholeheartedly with reckless abandon, and let the Love of your life know you are so glad to be one of His people.

*Lord, nothing makes my heart happier than knowing
You are with me. Please take me back one more
time to walk more closely with You. Amen.*

Please Hold!

Ask, and you will receive. Search, and you will find.
Knock, and the door will be opened for you. Everyone who
asks will receive. Everyone who searches will find. And the
door will be opened for everyone who knocks.
MATTHEW 7:7–8 CEV

God does not put you on *hold!* When you ask, when you knock, when you search for Him, He answers. Sometimes you may not recognize the answer, but the truth is, you are connected to God and He provides for your needs as quickly as possible.

If you're waiting for His answers, keep asking. Ask with all your heart and you will receive. Believe with everything you've got and you will receive. Knock louder than you've ever knocked before. Give God time to answer in the best way for you. Sometimes you and He have to work out the answer together.

Give Him a call. . .His line is open to you. He hears your heart already, and He never puts you on hold.

Lord, I am always knocking at Your door and I'm grateful
just to know You're in when I call. I'll wait humbly
for Your answers because only You know
what is best for my life. Amen.

I Don't Feel like Praying

We also pray that you will be strengthened with all his glorious power so you will have all the endurance and patience you need.
COLOSSIANS 1:11 NLT

Not in the mood to pray? Tapped out? Disillusioned? Maybe you simply feel like you don't know what more to say in prayer. Mother Teresa said this about prayer:

> Love to pray. Feel often during the day the need for prayer, and take the trouble to pray. Prayer enlarges the heart until it is capable of containing God's gift of Himself. Ask and seek and your heart will grow big enough to receive Him.

What a wonderful thought! Even when you're not feeling quite up to praying, the prayer itself will expand your heart so that you can receive all that God intends just for you. Your heart is all that's needed for real prayer to happen, for a connection to be made. God sees your heart before Him and comes to relieve, receive, and bless its desires.

Lord, prayer is about the heart relationship we share. Help me to love You so much that I bring everything to You in prayer no matter what mood I happen to be in at the time. Amen.

Who Can Stop the Rain?

The eyes of the L<small>ORD</small> watch over those who do right,
and his ears are open to their prayers.

1 P<small>ETER</small> 3:12 NLT

You may not have an interest in stopping the rain today, but you have a definite need for God to be with you, to open your heart, and to answer your fervent prayers. Keep your umbrella handy because you will receive what you pray for as long as your heart is ready to believe.

When you strive to live a heart-shaped life, you know that it's important to keep close to God and to do all you can to obey His guidance. He guides you out of love and out of a desire for you to both serve Him and have a personal relationship with Him. He guides you out of complete love and watches over you. Draw close to Him today. Who knows? He may even ask you to stop the rain with your prayers.

Lord, prayer has always been a mystery to me.
I know You're listening, so help my heart to be
open to pray about the right things. Amen.

Making Life Count

You should be happy to give the poor what they need, because then the LORD will make you successful in everything you do.
DEUTERONOMY 15:10 CEV

We want life to be about meaning, purpose, and the positive impact we can have on those around us. We don't necessarily want to be noted in history, but we'd like to feel deep within our own hearts that we made a difference. We want to feel successful in all we do.

God is gracious and gives us that opportunity every day. He provides for our needs and fills us up so we can open our hearts to others. We have a fulfilling and abundant life in Him each time we choose to share our hearts, skills, talents, and money with those around us.

You can make life count for someone today. Show them your goodness and compassion; show them your heart. You will surely make a difference!

Lord, I often think about those in need and do my best to help, but I know I don't do it enough. Please let me live more abundantly in Your service, and open my heart to the needs of those around me. Amen.

A Heart for the Lord

*There is one body and one Spirit, just as you were called to
one hope when you were called; one Lord, one faith,
one baptism; one God and Father of all.*

EPHESIANS 4:4–6 NIV

You may not recognize your value sometimes, but God always does. He knows that as He shapes your heart and mind, you'll get His work done. You're part of the family business and you signed up the day you accepted Jesus as your Lord and Savior.

Family businesses can go on for several generations or they can collapse in the first few months. What makes the difference is how well the family pulls together to get the job done. Each person has a unique role to play and it's very important to the success of the group.

You have a job to do and it begins with your heart. It is done in a way that helps others to see that Christ lives within you and that you are there to share His love. As an important member of His family, God blesses you because He counts on you!

*Lord, help me to be Your hands and feet today.
Help me to love others as You would love
them, wherever I am today. Amen.*

A Heart-Shaped Life

As long as he sought the LORD,
God gave him success.
2 CHRONICLES 26:5 NIV

We often believe that success has something to do with money, power, or position. We imagine having more material things indicates our level of worldly success. Perhaps, but what happens if we seek to rise to the level of God's measure of success?

If your goals are to leave the world a bit better than you found it, or share love so that you've warmed the heart of at least one other soul, then you can count yourself among the successful and among the blessed. As you seek the Lord, He will continue to give you glorious opportunities to succeed abundantly.

Lord, please continue to shape my heart to show Your
love, for that is where real success is found. Help me
to succeed in ways that please You today. Amen.

Finding the Rainbow

I have placed my rainbow in the clouds. It is the sign
of my covenant with you and with all the earth.

GENESIS 9:13 NLT

♥

Life is often flooded with sorrows and it can feel damp and gray. Your heart longs for the sunshine and the promise of better days ahead. You need a rainbow to help motivate your direction and get your heart back on course. You grow weary of being stuck in the same place, seemingly going nowhere, and having no means to create change.

You may well be stuck, but remember that God isn't! He's busy planning a future hope for you.

As you patiently wait for Him, open the doors to every opportunity to feel His presence. Pour out your concerns and let Him wash them away and create a bright new day for you. You will come upon your rainbow when you least expect it, and when your heart is fully prepared. Your Father has already placed it in the clouds.

Lord, it is so hard for me to wait for Your direction when
I'm anxious to make a change. Send me Your rainbow
today, and give me the heart to see it. Amen.

The Bear Went Over the Mountain

We live by believing and not by seeing.
2 CORINTHIANS 5:7 NLT

One of the songs from childhood is a silly song called "The Bear Went Over the Mountain." Now of course, we're not sure why the bear went over the mountain, but the song explains that he did so in order to "see what he could see."

Maybe it helps then if we "go over the mountain" before we can actually see all the great things that there are for us to discover. We have to look up into the hills from the valley and ask God to join us there. We have to look very intentionally for something new.

Walk in confidence, fully trusting God's plans for you. As He shapes your heart, He'll shape your thoughts and guide you to the landscape that will serve you the best. Believing is seeing.

Lord, Your goodness keeps me moving forward and keeps me looking up. Help me to cross through the valleys and up toward the peaks in faithfulness and joy. Amen.

No Pat Answers!

"Be strong and courageous!"
2 CHRONICLES 32:7 NLT

When a crisis hits you, there's only one real place to go. Take it to God and ask for His help. Share your heart with Him, seek His strength, and sit quietly in His presence. He will come and listen, and He will not try to give you any pat answers.

Be strong, courageous, and certain that He holds you powerfully in His hand. He cares more about you than anything in the world. He will help you in the ways that will serve your life and your spirit. When life throws you a curve, just duck, because God will be right there with a catcher's mitt.

Don't listen to anyone who tries to blame you or God for what has happened in your life. Trust that God knows your situation and is ready to comfort and bless you.

Lord, it is so wonderful to know that You are always there, and even in the midst of life's ups and downs, You hear my prayers. Be with me today, and give me strength and courage. Amen.

A Matter of Trust

I trust in God's unfailing love for ever and ever.
PSALM 52:8 NIV

If you put your trust in friends, your pastor, or your family, you may be on shaky ground. As soon as any one of them does something to let you down, moves away, or leaves you when you need them, your sense of trust may break down again.

If you put your trust in money or your job, you'll have to constantly protect those things because jobs can be lost and money disappears in ways you never expected.

You have only one place to dependably put your trust. God is the only one worthy of a lifetime of trust. You have to look up and let your Redeemer safeguard your heart, mind, and soul. In God we trust is more than a slogan for you; it's the one place to put your trust for today and always.

Lord, help me to know in my heart when to trust myself or when to trust others. Most of all, help me to build my trust in You today. Amen.

Right Choices! Wrong Choices!

We are the people he watches over, the flock under
his care. If only you would listen to his voice today!
The Lord says, "Don't harden your hearts."
PSALM 95:7–8 NLT

Living a heart-shaped life is about being willing to listen to God, surrender to His counsel, and let Him in to everything you do. You cannot develop a softer heart without seeking His voice for each decision and concern you have. You are pliable like soft clay when you are in His hands. That's the best place to be because He can shape you and remake your life into something beautiful, no matter what has gone on before.

A soft heart is not a weak heart! It's a heart that knows where its strength lies. It's a heart that rests solely in the care and keeping of Jesus. That's what you do each day, each morning when you surrender your life to Him so that He can tenderly watch over you.

Let the Holy Spirit guide your heart into the decisions you must make today.

Lord, I know if I'm making a decision that isn't healthy
or wise for myself, but I don't always have the strength
to step away from it. Please guide me with
Your love today. Amen.

No One Quite like You

Pay careful attention to your own work, for then you
will get the satisfaction of a job well done, and you
won't need to compare yourself to anyone else.
For we are each responsible for our own conduct.

GALATIANS 6:4–5 NLT

Humans love to compare things. We like to compare ourselves with others to gauge whether we're doing well. We push, we strive, we compete, over and over again.

This is one way to look at your life, but maybe there's a better way. Maybe you could appreciate the fact that God designed you as a unique individual with specific talents and an almighty purpose. Maybe you could align your heart more closely to God's to figure out how you're really doing.

He knows you well and wants you to feel pleased with your achievements. He wants you to strive to be more for Him, competing only with yourself because of your love for Him. After you do a little happy dance for the things you accomplished today, He wants you to move on and challenge your heart again to grow even bigger in His grace.

Lord, forgive me when I look to the world to figure out
whether I'm doing well or not. Help me to only look to
You for the measures of success that fulfills
Your purpose for me. Amen.

Your Worry Quotient

Give all your worries and cares to God,
for he cares about you.
1 PETER 5:7 NLT

Worry is one of those matters of the heart that often reflects your faith. If you believe God is taking care of you, then you know the basics are covered and you trust things are going okay. If you aren't sure if God is taking care of you, you're not sure anything is really covered. You hope it is, but you give in to worry just the same.

God will take care of you. In fact, He's always caring for you, and all you have to do is believe that He is. Nothing will come into your life that will surprise Him, and He will do all He can to help you with anything and everything. Raise your faith, not your doubts. Sweep out the worries and relax in God's care. Give your heart a rest today and let worry bother someone else.

Lord, it isn't easy to step aside from worry.
Help me to raise my faith and trust and believe
in You. My heart needs a rest. Amen.

The Last Straw

Don't worry about tomorrow. It will take care of itself.
You have enough to worry about today.
MATTHEW 6:34 CEV

Do you remember the scarecrow in the *Wizard of Oz*? When Dorothy first discovers him, he is hanging on the fence trying to figure out how to get down, which way to go, and hoping he won't fall apart in the process. The longer he hangs there, the surer he is that he'll never accomplish anything.

Dorothy gets him down from the fence and helps him pull himself together. She reminds him that he is great and just needs some direction and more confidence. Even though he isn't sure he's capable of making a decision, he follows Dorothy anyway.

If your worries have shaken you up like that, then stuff a little more faith into your system and take your shaky legs and walk toward God. He's ready even now to renew and strengthen you, and He'll gladly give you a new heart as well.

Lord, I need Your help to get my life together
now. Please renew my heart and my spirit,
and meet me on the path to direct my steps
toward Your will and purpose. Amen.

Too Smart to Be Wise?

Teach us to use wisely all the time we have.
PSALM 90:12 CEV

Proverbs 3:16–18 (CEV) talks about wisdom in the metaphor of an enlightened woman. It says this: "In her right hand Wisdom holds a long life, and in her left hand are wealth and honor. Wisdom makes life pleasant and leads us safely along. Wisdom is a life-giving tree, the source of happiness for all who hold on to her."

Wisdom provides a long life, and it's one that is pleasant and safe. Wisdom brings honor and substance. Wisdom is a source of happiness, a life-giving tree.

When you're trying to determine the best ways to follow your heart, it's good to seek truth and be aligned with God's plans for you. The fear or the adoration or the surrender of the spirit to God is the true beginning of wisdom.

This would be a simple word to the wise.

Lord, help me to seek Your wisdom in all that I do. Keep me ever connected to Your life-giving Source of all wisdom and grant me a more loving heart. Amen.

Listening with the Heart

If you love Wisdom and don't reject her,
she will watch over you.
PROVERBS 4:6 CEV

If part of wisdom is knowing when to keep quiet and when to speak up, we can appreciate the task set before us. Often, we speak up too quickly and later wish we had waited before sharing our thoughts. There's an old adage that says we have two ears and one mouth so we can listen twice as much as we speak.

Today, try listening with your heart. Let others have the floor and respond only as you must. Listen beyond the words, beyond the situation, and see if you can hear the truth of all the chatter going on around you. Listen the way you would hope God Himself would listen to you, with heartfelt sympathy and patience.

Lord, sometimes I'm so quick to get my thoughts on the table that I'm not very good at listening to those around me. Today, help me to be a thoughtful listener. Amen.

Peace from the Wild Side

The heavens declare the glory of God;
the skies proclaim the work of his hands.

PSALM 19:1 NIV

Wherever you live, you have opportunities to get out in nature, smell the fresh air, and walk among the flowers and foliage. Okay, some of you have to do this in a city park, but most of you can get away and enjoy creation as God intended it.

If you haven't experienced the good tidings coming your way from the mountaintops, or the freshness of the winds that clear out the noise in your head, then make today an opportunity to let God speak to your heart with clarity and power. You might be impressed with what you learn from the sound of a singing bird or the rippling waters of a creek bed. You may even hear the still, small voice of God speaking your name.

May His peace prevail in your heart today.

Lord, walk with me through the beauty of all
You've created, and speak to me in whispers that
only the mountains and rivers know at
every rising of the sun. Amen.

Your Job and Your Work!

Do your work willingly,
as though you were serving the Lord himself.
COLOSSIANS 3:23 CEV

♥

Your work is what you were born to do. For some people, it ties very closely to their chosen professions. For others, it's the work that feeds those around them in heart, soul, and mind through gifts of kindness, friendship, and love. It's the work you do for God, and so He always provides people in your midst who need to see His love in action. He brought you on for the job the day you asked Him to be your Savior. He has work that only you can do.

God loves it when you do your work, but He wants your heart to be reshaped in ways that allow you to volunteer your services. He's called you and delights in your service.

One thing is for sure, you'll never get laid off from His work.

Lord, help me to see all the work I do as something I do for
You. Bless those around me, and open opportunities
for Your work to continue everywhere. Amen.

Angel Sightings

Keep on loving each other as brothers and sisters.
Don't forget to show hospitality to strangers,
for some who have done this have entertained
angels without realizing it!

HEBREWS 13:1–2 NLT

We celebrate the work of angels during the Christmas season. We sing about them and honor them and delight in the part they played in the birth of Jesus. We hang angel ornaments on our Christmas trees and echo the words from old hymns, "Hark, the Herald Angels Sing" and others. It's a wonderful feeling to be blessed by God's messengers.

Follow the example of angels. Find a way that you might be an angel to someone else. Share a good word, do a kind deed, listen to someone else's concerns with a compassionate heart. As an angel in training, you might consider helping out in a nursing home, visiting children at the hospital, or bringing a gift to a shut-in. Playing angel has endless possibilities.

It's always a great time to share your heart by being an angel of love and peace. Look around, angels are everywhere!

Lord, help me to serve those in need in any way I can
every day of the year. Let me play "angel" for those
who may need to see You more clearly. Amen.

Glad Tidings!

Suddenly, an angel of the Lord appeared among them,
and the radiance of the Lord's glory surrounded them.
They were terrified, but the angel reassured them.
"Don't be afraid!" he said. "I bring you good
news that will bring great joy to all people."
LUKE 2:9–10 NLT

We don't use words like "glad tidings" much anymore apart from poetry, but we do talk about good news. We love to receive good news, and from our current worldview, good news is a pretty scarce commodity. It wasn't much different for the shepherds.

They lived with daily uncertainty. They protected their flocks from wolves and other predators. They wandered for miles looking for fresh water. They wondered when the Redeemer would be born and restore order to the world. They worked hard and faithfully tended to their daily routines while they waited for better days to come. What good news it must have been to them when they heard the angels singing of Christ's birth!

Today, consider ways you might share good news that will bring joy to those around you. It's your chance to do the work of angels.

Lord, we all look forward to the good news of Your saving
grace and love. Help us to work, live, and play with
the joy of knowing Your salvation. Amen.

At His Word

The Word became a human being and lived here with us. We saw his true glory, the glory of the only Son of the Father. From him all the kindness and all the truth of God have come down to us.

JOHN 1:14 CEV

The beauty of seeing Jesus as the "Word" is very powerful. The world was dark, hungry, and lonely. Then God sent the power of the Word to create newness, and His light came into the darkness in the form of a tiny baby.

As you sit in the quiet of your home, perhaps with dim lights twinkling around you, imagine the beauty and radiance that brought glory to the stars and light to the universe. Imagine the Word of God coming into your life to light up your heart forever.

At His word, God spoke life into the universe, and at His Word, Jesus speaks life into our very souls. Celebrate the Word in joy today!

Lord, what joy it brings to know that Your love lights up the universe and Your kindness fills the hearts of everyone who knows You as the Lord of lords. Amen.

Getting in the Spirit

*I was there and saw the Spirit come down on him like
a dove from heaven. And the Spirit stayed on him.*
JOHN 1:32 CEV

Imagine being there when Jesus was baptized, and the
visible Spirit of God anointed Him and was so real even
John could see it. Imagine that Spirit staying with Him,
and now feel that same Spirit calling your name, coming
closer to you, and living in your heart and soul.

Remember that the Spirit of all that is exists in and
through you. You are the smile that people will delight to
see. You are the gift that will be unwrapped with endless
love, and you are the heart of all that brings joy to your
heavenly Father. As you embrace His Spirit, know that
your spirit is totally aligned with the most powerful and
loving Spirit that ever will be!

*Lord, I am so grateful for Your love, and I thank
You for the amazing gifts and blessings
that are mine because of YOU. Amen.*

A Little Adoration

Shout praises to the LORD! With all my heart I will thank
the LORD when his people meet. The LORD has done many
wonderful things! Everyone who is pleased with God's
marvelous deeds will keep them in mind. Everything the
LORD does is glorious and majestic, and his
power to bring justice will never end.
PSALM 111:1–3 CEV

Open wide the door of your heart as you embrace your
friends and family and as you shine your light of love for
all to see.

If you're not someone who customarily is given to fits
of praise and adoration to God at any time of the year,
perhaps it's time to give in to the Spirit within you. Let
the windows of your spirit be raised up and your reflec-
tion of His love be seen everywhere you go. Thank God
for the blessings you've enjoyed through His grace. Take
some time with others to shout adoring praises to His
name!

God's gift to you was born into your heart a long time
ago; the baby in the manger is worthy of real celebration.
Give God the glory today!

Lord, I do give You the glory and thank You for the gifts
of joy, peace, and love that fill my life. I praise You,
Lord, for Your immeasurable kindness to me. Amen.

Love Is an Action Word

*Dear children, let us not love with words or speech
but with actions and in truth.*
1 JOHN 3:18 NIV

How do we understand the word *love*? What would love
in action feel like, taste like, or smell like? How can we
know if we are sharing love both in action and in truth?

Actions created in love feel good. They lift our spirits and encourage our hearts. If what you did yesterday
doesn't bring you peace of mind today, then try again.
Create meaningful interactions with the people around
you, and let love guide all you do. You can do it because
God put His Spirit of love within you.

God is love because He sent Jesus to redeem us.
You are love when you fit your words and your actions
together for His glory.

*Lord, let me show Your love to everyone I meet today.
Let me lift the spirits of others and strengthen
their hearts in each thing that I do. Amen.*

How Do You Quench Love?

Many waters cannot quench love, nor can rivers drown it.
If a man tried to buy love with all his wealth,
his offer would be utterly scorned.
SONG OF SONGS 8:7 NLT

God's love is forever unquenchable! You will never get enough of it and you will never use it up. Perhaps a way to capture a comparison is to think about someone in your life whom you truly love.

You may think that nothing could change the love that you have for this person and that you will always want more of it. You could never imagine that your love could dry up. You know that your love will continue to flow, flooding the heart of your beloved with every breath. It's amazing to think about this love. This thought may give you the initial flavor of God's outpouring of love for you.

Now think again about those dearest to your heart. Promise those you love that nothing will quench, or ever change, your love for them. May your love for others simply overflow.

Lord, let me overflow with love today, drinking You in,
breathing You out, so that everyone around me will
see more of You, less of me, and feel Your
unquenchable love. Amen

Put on a Happy Face

A happy heart makes the face cheerful,
but heartache crushes the spirit.
PROVERBS 15:13 NIV

Suffering, anguish, sadness, and other negative feelings come out of nowhere, ambushing you and leaving you feeling hopeless. The good news is that you don't have to embrace them. You don't have to carry them with you every place you go. In fact, you can't carry them because they are dead weights. Pray about your sorrow and then imagine putting it outside yourself, wrapping it up and just setting it aside. Ask Jesus to carry it for you, and then go out for a walk, unburdened.

Open your eyes to the world around you and focus your heart on the needs of others. Talk to a neighbor, reach out to a friend, and find a reason to laugh. By the time you return home, the burden you've been feeling will have lifted, your step will be lighter, and your face will shine with true joy.

Lord, help me to realize that my sorrows are important to
You and that I don't need to carry them alone. Amen.

Creating a Heart-Shaped Day

This is the day which the LORD has made;
let us rejoice and be glad in it.

PSALM 118:24 NASB

When you choose to view people as those that the Lord loves and has redeemed, and you choose to see life as a continual source of learning what is good, you'll be awake to the Spirit and able to see things in a more positive way. You'll see the light and not the darkness, the good and not the evil. Your heart will understand its purpose and shine a light through your smile and your kindness.

This is the day the Lord has made. It was created for you to enjoy right now. This is the only day you have; it's the gift of the present. When the sun goes down on this day, will you have spent it in joy? Will you be the reason someone else can rejoice? You are the light of the world and this is your day to shine. Rejoice!

Lord, as I walk in Your light, help me to bless everyone that comes onto my path with Your love and compassion. I offer You heartfelt thanks and praise in all things. Amen.

Living in Harmony

For God is not the author of confusion but of peace,
as in all the churches of the saints.

1 CORINTHIANS 14:33 NKJV

Harmony doesn't mean you have to sing the same note or even the same song as everyone else. It just means you have to hum along and help keep things running smoothly.

Your job for one conversation at a time, moment by moment, is to make today orderly. You will not allow discord, chaos, apathy, or anger, for these are all notes of discontent. The reason for great tension is often about the negative stories in your head, the ones you've allowed to have control. They don't have to have the last word though because you have other stories and they come from the love you have in your heart.

Let your song burst forth into praise for your God who loves you so and wants you to be at peace with everyone.

Lord, let me seek forgiveness from any that I may
have offended. Renew my heart and help me offer
friendship to those I meet today. Amen.

Love Truth and Peace

"Therefore love truth and peace."
ZECHARIAH 8:19 NIV

Because we always want those who are dear to us to feel important, we may not admit that we haven't thought about them lately. In our hearts, we really do mean to pray for people even when we forget. *"I'll call you"* is just a polite version of procrastination. . . at least sometimes. Those little "untruths" sneak into our lives all day long and before we know it, any sense of peace is gone.

What does it mean to love truth? Perhaps it means that you are proud of whatever you do today, that you operate with a heart that is considerate and kind and recognizes the needs of others, even placing those needs above your own. Peace comes when your heart is in the right place and your love is genuine. God has put His truth in your heart, and it is shaped by His grace to keep you coming back for more.

---

*Lord, You know my truth even better than I do.
Let me live in that truth and honor my friends and
family with my words and my intentions. Let me
seek real truth and peace today. Amen.*

The Wisdom of the Heart

*Real wisdom, God's wisdom, begins with a holy life
and is characterized by getting along with others.*
JAMES 3:17 MSG

Solomon asked God for wisdom to lead and rule over others. He was considered the wisest man of his day. What is wisdom? We may think the wisest people today are Rhodes Scholars or great scientists or inventors. We often equate wisdom with intellect or with being smart. We strive to be smarter than someone else, so we can stay slightly ahead of them. Does that mean we're wise?

The "wisdom of heaven" appears to be different though. It is about being considerate and showing mercy or kindness. It's about being peaceful and leading with a heart shaped by love. This kind of wisdom, the kind that brings inner peace, is the one for which we pray.

Today, may your loving heart guide you into true wisdom in all of your relationships.

*Lord, grant me the wisdom of a loving heart, the kindness
to extend to every living soul, and the mercy to realize
we all need Your grace each day. Help me to
live always in Your peace. Amen.*

Please Help Me Wait!

I wait for the LORD, my soul waits, and in His word
I do hope. My soul waits for the Lord more
than those who watch for the morning.
PSALM 130:5–6 NKJV

The psalmist stresses that waiting for the Lord requires even more patience than that of the watchman. The psalmist's soul longs for the Lord, living on the Word and passing the time in hope.

Most of us are neither the watchman, nor the psalmist. We don't have the patience to wait, night after night. You may recall that even Jesus couldn't get His disciples to wait with Him through that one lonely night in the garden.

Why do we grow weary of waiting so quickly? We pray for patience, but we want the waiting to be over now. Perhaps it is in the waiting where God can best shape our hearts to be more like His. Today, let us wait in anticipation, hope, and joy.

Lord, help me to wait in hope with Your Word to feed my
soul and Your grace to guide my spirit. Help me to
wait and not get ahead of You today. Amen.

The Patient Heart

Patient people have great understanding,
but people with quick tempers show their foolishness.
PROVERBS 14:29 NCV

There's often a fine line between impatience and folly. The old adage that "patience is a virtue" comes to mind here. The reason patience is a virtue is that we recognize we don't seem to have it programmed into us. We like things to happen quickly, because we live in an "on demand" kind of world. Few of us would claim that we're good at being patient or that we truly make the effort to gain understanding before we act. Hence, folly looms everywhere.

Another old saying is "The hurrier I go, the behinder I get!" It's amusing, but it's the reason that folly has so much opportunity in our lives. We resist the waiting and the planning and the things that would help us to move wisely.

May your heart be guided and gently shaped with greater patience in every task you undertake today.

Lord, rescue me from impatience. Help me to be willing
to listen, to seek to understand, and to simply give
things time to unfold according to Your will
and the plans You have for my life. Amen.

Be Kind to Your Soul

Your own soul is nourished when you are kind.
PROVERBS 11:17 TLB

God places a special premium on our efforts to be kind. The feedback for your effort lies in your own soul, for it feels nourished and your heart feels light. You are deeply aware of God's presence and you are able to share His light with confident joy.

How sad it is when we think that in order to succeed in the world, we have to be aggressive in our dealings with others, perhaps even abusive or hateful. What greater success could we have than being considered both kind and compassionate in all our dealings? Your soul delights in your kindness and your heart does a happy dance as well.

May your heart be blessed by the kind deeds you do at every opportunity.

Lord, fill my soul with joy today as I share my heart and mind with others according to Your grace and mercy. Let kindness be the rule and not the exception in all I do. Amen.

When Kindness Meets Love

We love because God loved us first. But if we say we
love God and don't love each other, we are liars. . . .
The commandment that God has given us
is: "Love God and love each other!"

1 JOHN 4:19–21 CEV

When God's Spirit works in our hearts, it blows the wind of kindness through our bodies and moves us into action. It fills us with a desire to be more loving and to literally become a source of inspiration and renewal for each other.

It demands that we show Jesus to everyone. It asks us to open our hands, lift up our hearts, and love like we may have never done before. We are brothers and sisters of His blood, and our heritage will take us through eternity. Let's love as He loved us.

Think of all the ways you love others. How can you create even more fulfilling and more loving relationships with everyone you know? God wants you to embrace each person in your life with His love and with amazing acts of kindness.

Lord, when I think of every person as being part
of Your family, it helps me to see each one more clearly,
through the eyes of my heart. Thank You for
Your amazing love for me. Amen.

Putting on the Glow

Light shines on those who do right;
joy belongs to those who are honest.
PSALM 97:11 NCV

Most of us like things to be shiny and clean. We wash an apple and dry it and make it shine before we eat it. We take a dust cloth and make the tabletop glow once again. We put on our best smile when we're going to meet a friend. We like to shine.

The reason God wants your light to shine is because the world has a lot of dark and dingy corners, places where few people even know a light exists. He wants you to share your heart and your light so that others can glow right along with you.

The best part of this is that your willingness to shine doesn't depend on the weather, your mood, or on the circumstances you might be in. It just depends on the strength of your relationship with God so that He can shine through you any time at all.

Shine on today!

Lord, help me to be mindful of Your presence
in all I do today so that I can help someone
else see Your light. Amen.

What Good Can You Do?

Serve wholeheartedly, as if you were serving the Lord,
not people, because you know that the Lord will
reward each one for whatever good they do.
EPHESIANS 6:7–8 NIV

What if you were walking along the street one day and you saw a sign that said, "$5000 reward for anyone caught in the act of doing good?" Would you pay special attention to doing good deeds for the rest of the day? Would you keep looking over your shoulder for the reward police to come along and give you the money? Would you try to outdo others in your acts of goodness?

Of course, it would be interesting to see how we would respond to such a sign, but then God has already posted that sign for us. He said He would give the gift of eternal life (a rather awesome reward) for all those caught in the act of believing in His Son.

When you serve others, you are serving Him. You have a chance every day to do His good deeds. Your reward is absolutely guaranteed!

Lord, help me to do good things for others without even
thinking about it. Make it such a natural part of me
to be an extension of You, that it's reward enough
to have had the privilege to do it. Amen.

Giving and Lending

But love your enemies, do good, and lend,
hoping for nothing in return; and your reward will
be great, and you will be sons of the Most High.
For He is kind to the unthankful and evil.

LUKE 6:35 NKJV

Did you ever stop to think about how kind God really is? On our worst days, when we've been selfish, inconsiderate, or grumpy to everyone we know, He is still kind to us. He doesn't demand that we let go of our frustrations or our anger or our bad hair days and just pretend they aren't happening. He hears us complain, and patiently waits in kindness for us to become more of the light He meant for us to be.

The good news is that God is giving and not lending. . . . He's not waiting for us to pay back before He gives more. He just keeps on giving.

Today, imagine that you have no interest in getting anything from anyone. All you need is an opportunity to be a giver, a giver with an amazing heart of love. May you give, and not even notice all you give, today.

Lord, help me to be more giving and less of a lender.
Help me to give freely without the need or thought of
getting something back. Let me give unconditionally,
fully, and clearly to those in need. Amen.

Guided Forever

For this God is our God for ever and ever;
he will be our guide even to the end.
PSALM 48:14 NIV

When you travel to an unfamiliar place and don't know the landscape or the best hotels and restaurants, you are apt to engage a tour guide or at least get a book or an app on the area to give you some direction so that you don't miss the best things about your adventure. It's more comfortable to know where you're going and what you can expect.

Psalm 48 is a reminder that you have the same opportunity for your travels across our planet. You have a God who has provided a Good Book to help you along the way. It's His personal GPS. He's ready to join you on the tour at any point you ask. He's prepared to show you new landscapes, and He'll stay with you until the whole trip is done.

Lord, help me travel today in the direction You would
have me go, whether it's across town or out of
the country. Please go before me and prepare
my heart for the journey. Amen.

According to Your Faith

When he had gone indoors, the blind men came to him,
and he asked them, "Do you believe that I am able to
do this?" "Yes, Lord," they replied. Then he touched
their eyes and said, "According to your faith let
it be done to you"; and their sight was restored.
MATTHEW 9:28–30 NIV

Most of us are not blind in the literal sense of the word. We can fumble for our glasses and get the right perspective of the world pretty quickly. We can get through the day without running into walls. . .or can we?

If Jesus could stand in front of you and answer a desire of your heart "according to your faith," would it happen? Would you overcome your own spiritual blindness enough to see His amazing grace for you?

Faithfulness requires us to believe that Jesus can restore our misty thoughts, our dark sides, and our uncertainties. He can shape our hearts to see Him more clearly and to see others with greater understanding and love. May Jesus touch some area of blindness in your life and shed His light on your darkness so that you may see His hand at work in your daily life. May His will be done "according to your faith."

Lord, You know that my faithfulness wavers.
Shape my heart today to be faithful and to be
willing to overcome my own blind spots. Amen.

A Heart-Shaped Spirit

"So now I am giving you a new commandment:
Love each other. Just as I have loved you, you should
love each other. Your love for one another will prove
to the world that you are my disciples."

JOHN 13:34–35 NLT

We all make promises to ourselves—and sometimes even to God—to live better lives. We promise we'll pray more, love more, or give more. . . . We truly hope to be better people, more aware of what motivates our thoughts and causes us to rejoice in life's goodness.

God always hears those promises and blesses the spirit in which we make them. He knows that right at that moment, we really mean to follow through. He knows we have good intentions to do better today than we did yesterday.

Perhaps today, you can really step into the world heart-first. Seek more of His Spirit to help you keep those heartfelt promises. Keep aligning yourself with God's direction, asking for a clean heart and a new way to share His love. Ask Him to give you the kind of eyes that focus on all that it means to love wholeheartedly.

As I open the door to a new day, Lord, strengthen and
renew my joy, my love, and my commitment to You. Amen.